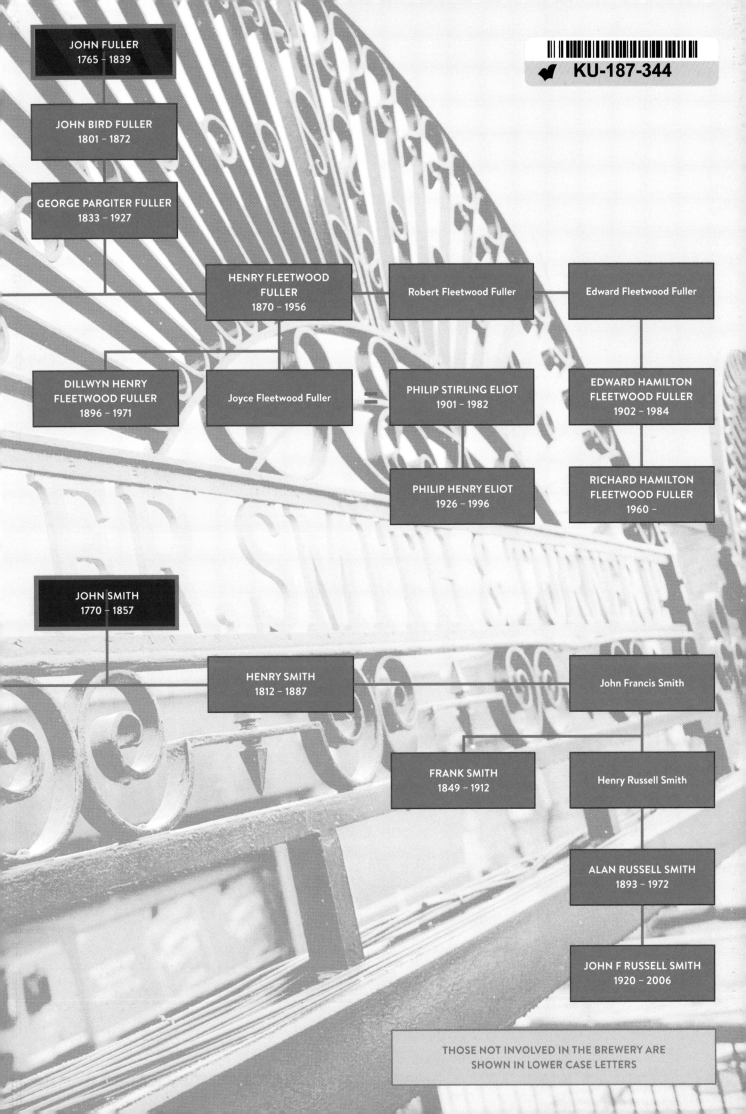

JOHN FULLER
1765 – 1839

JOHN BIRD FULLER
1801 – 1872

GEORGE PARGITER FULLER
1833 – 1927

HENRY FLEETWOOD FULLER
1870 – 1956

Robert Fleetwood Fuller

Edward Fleetwood Fuller

DILLWYN HENRY FLEETWOOD FULLER
1896 – 1971

Joyce Fleetwood Fuller

PHILIP STIRLING ELIOT
1901 – 1982

EDWARD HAMILTON FLEETWOOD FULLER
1902 – 1984

PHILIP HENRY ELIOT
1926 – 1996

RICHARD HAMILTON FLEETWOOD FULLER
1960 –

JOHN SMITH
1770 – 1857

HENRY SMITH
1812 – 1887

John Francis Smith

FRANK SMITH
1849 – 1912

Henry Russell Smith

ALAN RUSSELL SMITH
1893 – 1972

JOHN F RUSSELL SMITH
1920 – 2006

THOSE NOT INVOLVED IN THE BREWERY ARE
SHOWN IN LOWER CASE LETTERS

# CRAFTING A COMPANY

## HOW FULLER, SMITH & TURNER BECAME LONDON'S ICONIC BREWERY

WRITTEN BY ADRIAN TIERNEY-JONES

ADAPTED FROM *LONDON PRIDE*, WRITTEN BY ANDREW LANGLEY

# CONTENTS

# FOREWORD

## BY MICHAEL TURNER, CHAIRMAN

I AM DELIGHTED to be able to write a foreword to this book on behalf of all the many families (not just those of the founders) who have worked in the company for several generations, and who have made it what it is today. We are lucky to be in an industry that we all enjoy as it leads to great job satisfaction.

I am often asked what the secret of the company's enduring success is down to. It is most importantly as a result of great teamwork, with everyone in the company having a desire to produce their best, and a collective pride in our success. This happens because everyone shares a clear vision of where we need to get to, and what we need to do to get there and it is all done with values that we are proud of.

The role of the team is to be the guardians of our wonderful business, growing and enhancing it for future generations of employees and shareholders, and that means having a long-term strategy that often requires patience. Investing in the long term means that you can't cut corners by using cheaper ingredients or cutting service levels. Such actions are seductive in the short term and boost profits but in the long term they damage the brand and the magic is lost.

Ours is a business that has grown and prospered over time by identifying niches where we can play to our strengths and add value by concentrating on quality above all else, and by being professional, inventive, original, creative and fun.

The company has a rich history and heritage but we spend our time looking forward at the challenges of tomorrow rather than basking in the successes of the past. When the company was formed it was one of several thousand breweries in the London area, but we are the last survivor of all of them, and are excited to be leading the capital's thriving new craft brewing scene.

A key for us is a culture of style not fashion. We feel style is enduring whilst fashion is transient. The trends in business change regularly, and in the past we were frequently told that our business model of being a vertically integrated brewer was outdated, that we should be either a brewer or a pub retailer, that we should run either tenancies or managed houses, but not both, we should not be in hotels, and that our balance sheet was inefficient. The big companies of the day such as Bass, Whitbread, Courage, Allied, Watneys, Scottish and Newcastle, Vaux, Greenall Whitley and countless others listened to the advice and sadly are no more. Because of our family shareholding and an unshakeable vision of where we wanted to go, we were able to ignore the advice and the criticism to the point where now, with the benefit of hindsight, the City hold us up as having the ideal business model.

I will finish by looking to the future, where the pace of change offers us so many opportunities such as our purchases of Gales Brewery, Cornish Orchards cider and The Stable cider and pizza business have proved in the past. If we all continue to work together as a team, upholding our values, our culture, our creativity, our originality, our family atmosphere and our operational excellence, then the future of this wonderful company will be exciting and, most importantly, fun to work in.

I hope you enjoy this book. It is not just a record of where we have come from, but also a snapshot of the present and a glimpse into the future. And that future is looking very positive from here.

# CHAPTER ONE

# To Begin At The Beginning

HERE IS A BREWERY with the aroma of the boil suffusing the air, sweet and bitter, warm and comforting, where the hand of tradition that has pervaded this site for centuries can be felt. A tangle of wisteria smothers an outside wall, the clang of metal casks rings out from somewhere in the building and a man in orange overalls buzzes by in a fork-lift truck. The everyday business of brewing and running a brewery is underway.

Inside the brewery, up the steps, there stands a collection of stainless steel vessels, some conically shaped at the base, while others are survivors from an older time, wood and gleaming copper, a sugar dissolver, an ancient mash tun, stationary and silent now, signposts on the way beer used to be brewed.

Throughout the three floors of activity, members of the brewing fraternity stand and check, swirl themselves about the fermenting vessels, sit down in front of computers and watch a stream of numbers that tell the story of the day's work.

This is Fuller, Smith & Turner on a busy working day, when thousands of gallons of London Pride, ESB, Black Cab Stout and Frontier (to name but a few) are being brewed and conditioned and led to their ultimate destination: the glass of the beer lover. Though this beer will end up either in a pub cellar or reside in bottle, a very special elite is currently sleeping the sleep of the just within whisky casks, safely ensconced in one corner of this busy brewery.

Who knows, perhaps someone, somewhere, within this building and bustling enterprise is thinking of those

who went before them; those who brewed beer, sold beer, drank beer, breathed beer; those who make up the series of human dramas that clamour for our attention whenever we think of the past. Let us now try to find some of those people lurking behind the curtains and folds of yesterday.

BEER AND BREWING HISTORY have a habit of concealing themselves within a maze of myths and legends. Take porter, for instance – until recently this classic beer of the 18th century was thought to have emerged through the actions of one man, Ralph Harwood. However, research in the last couple of decades has shown that the truth is far more complicated. The same has occurred with other classic beer styles such as India pale ale, stout and, fast-forwarding into the modern age, black IPA. It does seem that classic beer styles evolved, somehow, accidentally perhaps, but not in a way suggestive of a beery Archimedes jumping out of the bath and running down the street proclaiming that porter or India pale ale had been discovered.

A similar fog lies deep and opaque over the exact date that brewing first began in Chiswick. The chances are that from the Middle Ages onwards (when Chiswick was a small fishing village centred upon the church of St Nicholas), both those living in cottages as well as in manor houses would have made their own ale, as was the fashion then (with many of the brewers being women, or brewsters as they were known). However, when we get to the year of the Spanish Armada light is let in and we have a solid record of brewing in Chiswick. Thanks to a lease dated 16 December 1588,

CORNEY HOUSE, CHISWICK, AS IT WAS IN 1760. A BREWHOUSE ON THE CORNEY ESTATE IN THE 16TH CENTURY MARKS THE BEGINNING OF THE BREWING INDUSTRY IN CHISWICK

we know that one William Holden took out a lease 'on a Brewhouse, Horsemill and Chambers at Chiswick… for five years at 40/- per year'.

This brewhouse was located on the Corney House estate, which was roughly half a mile west of the present Griffin Brewery, close to the banks of the Thames. And the beer that was brewed?

According to Martyn Cornell in *Beer: The Story of the Pint*, 'the main beer styles of Elizabethan England seem to have been single beer and double beer', with the former being the weaker variety. In the same book, Cornell writes about the tradition of the gentry and nobility brewing a March beer, which as the name suggests was brewed in the month of March (before warmer temperatures made brewing difficult) and was usually aged for at least a year, and sometimes two years.

Corney House would no doubt have been amply supplied with ale, a situation that must have been a happy bonus for the owner Sir William Russell when Elizabeth I paid a visit in 1602. One hopes that the Queen (for Russell's sake), who disliked strong ale (and presumably would have turned down the offer of a glass of March beer), did not have a repeat of an earlier occasion, when she visited a house in Oxfordshire in the summer of 1575. As her travelling companion, the Earl of Leicester, related in a letter afterwards: 'Being a marvellous hot day at her coming, there was not

one drop of good drink for her… her own here was so strong as there was no man able to drink it; you had been as good to have drunk Malmsey. It did put her far out of temper.'

BY THE END OF THE 16TH CENTURY, home brewing was starting to decline with the emergence of commercial brewers, or what were called 'common brewers' (though the practice of large country houses having their own brewery continued into the late 19th century and indeed has been revived in recent years). There were other changes afoot. The old-fashioned 'ale', made simply of water, yeast and malt, and often with spices and herbs added, had a competitor in the shape of 'beer', a hopped beverage that was introduced into England by Flemish immigrants in the 15th century, who initially brewed it for their own community. The hops not only added a delicious and much-needed bitterness to the flavour; they also improved the keeping qualities of the brew. This encouraged the common brewers to expand their businesses and deliver further afield. As beer gradually overtook ale in popularity, so the common brewers began to replace

16TH-CENTURY BREWING SAW THE EMERGENCE OF COMMERCIAL BREWERS

# CHISWICK IN THE 18TH CENTURY

AFTER FULLER'S, perhaps the most famous name to be associated with Chiswick is the satirist and artist William Hogarth, whose former house (now a museum) is a few minutes' walk from the brewery. He moved to the area in 1749 and died in 1764. Along with his wife Jane, he is buried in St Nicholas' churchyard. It's probable that he enjoyed the beers from the brewery and perhaps his *Beer Street* engraving (a counterblast to *Gin Lane*) was influenced by the enjoyment of the local brews when Matthew Graves was in charge of matters.

the domestic brewers. You could argue that the 16th century not only marked the end of the medieval world in what we now call modern Europe, but it also saw a similar change in brewing practice.

The growth of common brewers was accompanied by a governmental interest in brewing, which wasn't about what was in the glass. Brewing began to be seen as a source of revenue, something that has continued down the centuries. In 1614, James I imposed a tax of four pence to be paid every quarter on all malt used by brewers in London. When the Civil War broke out in 1642, both Charles I and the Parliamentarians raised revenue for their rival armies by slapping duty on beer itself. Although intended as a temporary measure, this tax was not lifted until 1850. Despite it, the common brewers continued to grow at the expense of their smaller competitors.

The English Civil War came to Chiswick in 1642 at the Battle of Turnham Green, when a Royalist force was blocked from advancing on London by a Parliamentarian army. Thankfully, this was the only military action in the area (an intriguing footnote is that two of Oliver Cromwell's daughters are buried in St Nicholas). Meanwhile, on the brewing front it is known that by the time of the Restoration in 1660 there were at least two brewhouses in Chiswick.

Bedford House, which had been built for the Earl of Bedford at the west end of Chiswick Mall, was now the home of the Russell family (Sir Michael Redgrave of the acting dynasty owned it from 1945 to 1954). A lease of January 1661 describes it as including a 'dove house, brewhouse, orchard, pond and five gardens' and with 'those two messuages [a dwelling with land and outbuildings] adjoining being converted and made into a brewhouse and other necessary outhouses'. This stood at the rear of Bedford House, with a passageway leading to Chiswick Lane. When Edward Russell died in 1665, the estate was sold to one Thomas Plukenett.

Meanwhile, a rather humbler concern was operating nearby, where Thomas Urlin and his wife lived in a modest cottage at the Mall end of Chiswick Lane. The hearth tax returns for 1671 stated that Urlin had '5 hearths and 1 brew chimney' (this tax was imposed in 1662 to help pay for the royal court's expenses, but was discontinued in 1689). The latter was on land south of the passageway leading to Bedford House, with Chiswick Lane to the east and Brick Lane to the north. Sadly, there is little historical evidence that can tell us how successful Urlin was, what kind of beers he was producing and if they were popular with local drinkers. However, we do know that when he died in 1682 his business passed to his widow and son-in-law, so his brews must have been drinkable at the very least.

Now that the mists are starting to clear ever so slightly, let's repair to the Mawson Arms, which stands on the corner of the brewery, and enjoy perhaps a glass of Seafarers or London Pride. It's a popular pub both with Fuller's workers – the brewery's current head brewer, John Keeling, remembers that this was where he had a pint of Chiswick on his first day of work back in 1981 – and visitors; brewery tours start from here. This is the brewery tap, the closest place to Fuller's where you can drink its beers. It is also an ideal place to toast the memory of a key figure in the history of the Griffin Brewery.

The pub is named after Thomas Mawson, an ambitious soul who arrived in Chiswick in the 1680s and proceeded within two decades to lay the foundations for a major brewing enterprise. First of all, he started as manager for the widow Urlin but, by 1699, he had bought up her equipment and leased 'one cottage, five tenements, two orchards and a garden' on the site.

Expansion was rapid. In search of pubs to sell his beer, Mawson soon purchased the George public house (now the Fuller's-owned Grade II-listed George and Devonshire), plus two adjoining cottages for £70. In 1701, he bought the Bedford House brewhouse from the Plukenetts, later uniting the two properties by acquiring the slip of land used as a passageway between them. The premises of the present brewery were beginning to take shape.

When Thomas Mawson died in 1714 at the age of 58, he was described as a 'rich brewer'. Just how rich may be judged from his will. To his eldest son, Thomas, went the brewery (after his widow's death), including 'malthouse, brewhouse, stables and outhouses together with making utensils, coppers, backs and tunns and other utensils'. To his second son, Matthias, he left his estate in the manor of Sutton Court and freehold house in Chiswick. His third son, Benjamin, received land in Acton, four houses on Turnham Green and two in Chiswick village, and his youngest son, William, three houses and two barns in Chiswick, the King's Head, and land in Ealing.

Sadly, neither Benjamin nor William Mawson were able to enjoy their inheritances for long as they died young, while Matthias swapped the pub for the pulpit when he chose to follow a distinguished career in the church. So it was Thomas junior who carried on the brewing business alone, and when his energy, or enthusiasm, waned in 1740, he leased the premises to another local brewer, William Harvest of Brentford. The term 'Hock' survives to this day in the Hock Cellar at Fuller's, while one of its occasional beers has been Hock, a dark mild common to London. During the 18th century, Hock, which was an old English word for harvest, was applied to harvest ales.

Thomas Mawson junior died in 1748, leaving his brewery interests to brother Matthias, who by now was Bishop of Chichester and would later become Bishop of Ely as well as benefactor of Corpus Christi College, Cambridge. For this reason, Matthias had no working interest in the brewery, and it was now that another and more dynamic personality stepped in. Enter Matthew Graves, an affluent solicitor of the Inner Temple, who was in search of a lucrative business venture in which to invest. He foresaw that the brewing industry was heading for a boom, and promptly took on the lease of Mawson's property (retaining Harvest as brewer). The shrewd Graves also realised that selling beer was just as important as making it. He began leasing inns in the Chiswick area, paying £200 for the Coach and Horses on Turnham Green and going on to acquire, among others, the Red Lion at Acton, the Catherine Wheel at Brentford, the Bull's Head at Strand-on-the-Green and the Three Jolly Gardeners at Hammersmith. These were added to existing outlets for the brewery, owned or leased by the Mawson family, and including the Fox and Dogs in Chiswick and the Barge Aground at Brentford.

Bishop Mawson died in 1770 and the property was bequeathed to his niece. She in turn passed her interests on to her son, Charles Purvis. Meanwhile, Graves

CONTEMPORARY VIEW OF AN 18TH-CENTURY LONDON BREWHOUSE ILLUSTRATING A LABOUR-INTENSIVE INDUSTRY

continued to build up his estate. In 1777, he became tenant of the Red Lion Inn and eight adjoining cottages in Chiswick Lane and Chiswick Mall. This was the last 18th-century acquisition, completing the east half of the present brewery premises.

Three years later, in 1780, the *Gentleman's Magazine* recorded the death of Matthew Graves at the age of 69, describing him as a brewer. In his will, Graves rather whimsically stipulated that the brewhouse should go on operating for a further two years 'and no longer, and then I do order the same to be disposed of'. Thus it came about in 1782 that the brewery, with its web of different freeholds and copyholds, was put on the market again.

That autumn a 'rest' or inventory of the entire Graves estate was drawn up. It paints a vivid picture of the establishment and its hardware:

*The Cooper's Shop:*
the cooper's tools; 500 rivets; 200 Twopenny Nails; one Pewter Crane; 1 old bad Crane and 1 old Grindstone and Trough.

*The Counting House:*
1 Wainscoat Desk; 1 Iron Chest; 1 Poker, Shovel, Tongs and Grate; 1 Windsor Chair; ½ Pint Silver Pot; 1 Stool; 1 Pewter Ink Stand.

*The Tun Room:*
Yeast Stands; 5 Copper Filing Kettles; 216 foot of Old Leather Pipe; 3 Brass Screws; 92 foot of Good Leather Pipe.

*Upon the Stage:*
Tubs and Hoops.

*The Malt Loft:*
2 Old Bushel Measures; 1 Malt Screen; 1 Plank; 1 Old Shovel.

*The Yards:*
9 old Stinking Butts unhead'd; 3 old Stinking Puncheons; 3 old Stinking Barrells; 1 Old Boar;

3 Old Sows; 2 Good Piggs; 10 Young Piggs.

*The Coach House and Stable:*
1 Puncheon Binn, Lock and Key; 1 Water Butt Tub.

*Dray Horse Stable:*
Tubs and Hoops; 3 Dung Forks; 3 Old Shovels; a Parcel of Chalk.

*The Stoker Room:*
1 old Bed; 1 Blankett; 1 Quilt; 1 Table; 1 Chair.

*Coopers' Lobby:*
Barrell Stands; 1 Hair Sieve; 1 Burning Iron; 1 Cork Basket.

*Coopers' Room:*
1 Old Binn; 2 Quart Copper Pots; 1 Gallon Vitriol; 36lbs Ising Glass.

*Hop Loft:*
2 Old Shovels; 1 Pair Scales with 4...56lbs, 2...28lbs, 2...14lbs, 2...7lbs, 2...2lbs, 1...1lb weights; 3 dozen and 6 Brooms; 3 old Ropes; 6 Coal Sacks.

*Cash in Counting House*...£998-0-0.
*Total valuation of Brew House*...£63-0-0.
*Entire valuation of the Estate*...£10,273-12-8.

This assemblage of barrels, livestock and leather piping hardly sounds like the basis for amassing a fortune. Yet the down-to-earth mundanity of the inventory is misleading; at this point in the 18th century, brewing was very big business in London. This was also the age of porter, a style of beer that was brewed across the British Isles, though London porter had the best reputation. In the previous year, 1781, Thrale's Brewery in Southwark had been sold on the owner's death for £135,000. Samuel Johnson, who was a close friend of the widow, had helped with the transaction, glorying in the unaccustomed role of entrepreneur. When asked the value of the property, he had loftily replied: 'We are not here to sell a parcel of boilers and vats, but the potentiality of growing rich beyond the dreams of avarice.'

If they had read it, Johnson's statement would have probably drawn a hollow laugh from the two prospective purchasers of the Chiswick breweries. John Thompson, a maltster, and David Roberts, a distiller, quickly found themselves knee-deep in a morass of litigation and conveyancing. Having agreed to pay the asking price of £10,273, they were confronted by unexpected demands from the Graves family. It appeared that George, Graves' son, would not reach his 21st birthday until 1787, and was therefore entitled to all the rents until then. Thompson and Roberts fought the claim. The case dragged through the Court of Chancery, where it was eventually settled in George's favour. The purchasers had to pay over an additional £5,746.

Meanwhile, the solicitor acting for Thompson and Roberts was having great difficulty in drawing up a single conveyance from the mass of title deeds to the various other properties. He was not helped by the fact that the Mawson family vault stood on the land. There was much fretting lest the new owners should disturb the bones and coffins.

In 1786, David Roberts withdrew from the partnership, and also relinquished his share. Ironically enough, his reason for bailing out was not frustration with all the problems they had encountered. He had been appointed to the Household of King George III at Kew Palace, where he was to teach the Queen and the royal children drawing, English and handwriting. This plum job meant that he had to renounce all connections with vulgar 'trade'.

So John Thompson soldiered on alone, and for several years the brewery flourished. Catastrophe, however, was not far away (and let's not forget that we are also entering the period of the Napoleonic Wars, which had a detrimental effect on British brewing trade in Europe, especially the Baltic). Although Thompson himself

REID'S OLD GRIFFIN BREWERY IN CLERKENWELL, CIRCA 1820. THE GRIFFIN NAME WAS PURLOINED BY THE THOMPSON BROTHERS AND BECAME THE SYMBOL FOR THE CHISWICK BREWERY

# LIQUID ASSETS

IT USED TO BE SAID THAT BRITISH BREWERS used water for cleaning their vessels and pipes, but 'liquor' is utilised for making beer. Both, of course, are $H_2O$ and very few brewers, large, medium or small, would be so pedantic today. Needless to say, a particular quality of water/liquor is essential for making good beer. Burton-on-Trent became a brewing centre because of the quality of its water and many brewers moved there. By the late 19th century, brewers had discovered that they could replicate Burton-on-Trent's famous liquor by adding various salts to their own. This process is called Burtonisation and is still in use by many brewers – the main salts involved are gypsum (calcium sulphate) and Epsom salts (magnesium sulphate). Soft water is usually good for lagers (the soft waters of Plzen, for example, are just right for making Pilsner Urquell), whereas hard water, with its abundance of minerals, is good for bitter. London was always famed for its hard waters, with John Keeling explaining that 'the reason why we make such good porters and stouts is the chloride and sodium content in the water'. This possibly explains why porter is the beer style most associated with the city.

# TASTING NOTE
## LONDON PORTER, 5.4%

DURING THE 18TH CENTURY, porter was the beer that transformed the fortunes of many brewers in London, though Fuller's, as it would become known, would not brew it until the middle of the 19th century when the beer was on the wane. This is the brewery's modern version of the beer style that irrevocably is a London beer. It was first brewed in 1996 and, according to John Keeling, 'we had released 1845 to coincide with the 150th anniversary of the Fuller, Smith & Turner partnership and it had been a real success. We needed another beer to follow on from this and so we looked back again into our past. London is the spiritual home of porters and we are a London brewery.' Until 2000 it was an export-only brand but, after winning a gold medal in the Beer and Cider category in 1999's International Food and Drink competition, it went on release in its home country in bottle only (though it's also now available on keg).

Chestnut brown in colour, it has a creamy, treacle-toffee nose, with a hint of hop in the background; it's creamy and toffee-like on the palate, with a smooth mouth feel, bitter notes in the finish and a dryness that encourages another sip. There's a chewiness in its texture and shape, which contrasts with its silky creaminess. This is modern porter at its very best.

appears to have been a man of the utmost probity, there was a shady element in his wife's family, which was to bring the business close to ruin. The first hint of this had come in an apparently irrelevant episode in 1780, when Captain Henry Byrne (Thompson's brother-in-law) had been lost at sea in a hurricane. In the aftermath, Thompson set himself the task of sorting out Byrne's affairs. He was astonished to discover that the late captain had been a highly organised smuggler of woollen goods, with a network of 'ladies' in various trading ports who sold on his contraband. The strain of dishonesty was to surface in the next generation, most notably in Thompson's two sons – Douglas and Henry.

This pair took over the brewery when their father died in 1807 and managed to get the business to run smoothly. Sales and production increased and in 1816 the brothers bought Newton's Brewery and 11 public houses in Brentford, Isleworth and Norwood Green. They did this with the aid of a mortgage of £18,000 from one Thomas Harrington. That same year also saw the first appearance of the name 'Griffin Brewery' in Chiswick. The Griffin had for several years been the symbol of Meux and Reid's Brewery in Liquorpond Street (which is now part of Clerkenwell Road). When that partnership broke up in raucous circumstances in 1809, Douglas pinched the name, which has been retained ever since (though the Griffin trademark was not officially granted until 1892).

Things began to go wrong in 1821. Douglas Thompson's first wife died, and shortly afterwards he married Hannah Hill. For this happy event, he had to provide a marriage settlement of £300 a year. But where was he to find it? Without blinking – and without telling his brother – Douglas took out another mortgage on all the brewery premises, this time for £6,000, over a period of 500 years. The marriage was soon blessed with a son, who was christened, ominously, with the family name of Byrne.

Henry, meanwhile, had also begun taking out extra mortgages in order to purchase or lease more public houses. Naturally, he neglected to inform Douglas. By 1826 the Thompson brothers were in trouble. They must have defaulted on the main mortgage payments to Thomas Harrington, for they were forced to surrender various copyholds to him. To their horror, Harrington and the other mortgagees discovered that many of the properties were worth much less than they had been told.

The brothers had claimed, for example, that the Black Horse at Greenford had been bought freehold. In fact, it was only copyhold, which made a considerable difference to its value. Henry and Douglas were given six months to extricate themselves from the sale; if not, they would be accused of fraud.

Needless to say, there was no money available for the refund. It had all been lost on other ventures. As the pressure mounted, the extent of Henry's double-dealing was revealed. He had routinely pushed up the valuations of properties to ridiculous levels in order to get bigger mortgages. Now, he was unable to meet the repayment demands. Retribution and ruin stared the Thompsons in the face.

Yet somehow they stayed out of the courts and somehow the brewery continued to survive. Indeed Henry, in a bitter letter to his brother, claimed that he alone had managed to increase sales from 8,000 barrels in 1807 to 24,000 barrels in 1828. The squabbling intensified, but the Thompsons still had enough cunning to search for a way out of their predicament.

Money was needed and plenty of it. They approached Philip Wood, a member of an old-established family of hop merchants and brother of London's Lord Mayor, and invited him to become a partner. It did not take Wood long to realise that even his wealth was not enough to save the business. He, in his turn, approached a country gentleman in Wiltshire and proposed that he too should enter the partnership. The cavalry had been called and the name of the man leading the charge was John Fuller.

# PERFECT WITH FULLER'S LONDON PORTER

# Steak and Oyster Suet Pie with Peppered Hispi Cabbage and Mashed Potato

Serves 4

## INGREDIENTS

3 tbsp   plain flour

salt and freshly ground black pepper

1kg      chuck steak (a great cut
         for slow cooking), cut into
         3cm cubes

vegetable oil, for frying

30g      butter

1        medium onion,
         finely chopped

1        garlic clove, crushed

1 tsp    tomato purée

200ml  Fuller's London Porter

1.5 litres hot beef stock

1 tsp    chopped thyme leaves

1        small bay leaf

½ tsp    cornflour (if needed)

8        large oysters, shucked

### For the pastry:

225g     self-raising flour,
         plus extra for dusting

1 tsp    salt

85g      shredded beef suet

60g      butter, chilled and diced

1        medium free-range egg,
         beaten, to glaze

## METHOD

Season half of the flour with salt and pepper and use to lightly flour the meat. Heat a little oil in a large, heavy-based frying pan and fry the meat in two or three batches over a high heat until nicely browned. Set aside on a plate. Melt the butter in a large, heavy-based pan or flameproof casserole and fry the onion and garlic for a few minutes until lightly coloured. Add the remaining flour and tomato purée. Stir over a low heat for a minute or so, then slowly add the porter and hot stock, stirring to avoid lumps forming. Add the steak with the thyme and bay leaf. Heat through, cover and simmer very gently for about 2 hours until the meat is tender. When the meat is cooked, the sauce should have thickened to a gravy-like consistency. If not, mix a little cornflour to a paste with 1 tablespoon water, stir into the sauce and simmer, stirring, for a few minutes. Leave to cool. Set some of the gravy aside for pouring over the pie.

To make the pastry, mix the flour, salt, suet and butter together in a large bowl and make a well in the centre. Mix in enough water (about 150ml) to form a smooth dough and knead for a minute. Roll the pastry out on a floured surface to a thickness of 7–8mm. Cut out four discs to make pie bases and the same for lids (the bases should be twice the size of the lids), about 2cm larger all round than the pie dishes. Insert the pastry bases in the pie dishes. Brush the edges of the pastry with a little of the beaten egg. Spoon the cooled filling into the 4 individual pie dishes (or you could use one large dish, if you prefer) to about 1cm from the rim. Pop the shucked oysters in the centre, 2 in each. Lay the pastry lids over the filling, pressing the egg-washed sides on to the rim of the base pastry dishes. Cut a 2cm hole in the centre to allow steam to escape. Rest in a cool place for 30 minutes. Preheat the oven to 200°C/fan oven 180°C/gas mark 6. Brush the pies with beaten egg and bake for 30–35 minutes (or 40–50 minutes for a large one) until the pastry is golden.

Continued on following page...

# PERFECT WITH FULLER'S LONDON PORTER

## Steak and Oyster Suet Pie with Peppered Hispi Cabbage and Mashed Potato (Continued)

INGREDIENTS

**For the mash:**

680g  Yukon Gold potatoes, peeled and quartered

½ tsp  salt

30g  butter

60ml  double cream

1 tbsp  milk (or more)

**For the hispi cabbage:**

1  cabbage

100g  butter

METHOD

To make the mash, place the potatoes in a medium saucepan and add enough cold water to cover the potatoes by at least 2.5cm. Add the salt and bring to the boil over a high heat. Reduce the heat to low, cover and simmer for 15–20 minutes, or until you can easily poke through the potatoes with a fork.

While the potatoes are cooking, melt the butter and warm the cream. You can heat them together in a pan on the stove or in the microwave. When the potatoes are done, drain the water and place the steaming hot potatoes in a large bowl. Pour the heated cream and melted butter over and mash the potatoes with a potato masher. Then use a strong wooden spoon (a metal spoon might bend) to beat further. Add the milk and beat until the mashed potatoes are smooth. Don't over-beat or the mash will end up gluey. Season to taste.

Prepare the hispi cabbage by cutting it in half and removing the core root. Then cut into ribbons and rinse under cold water. Set aside. Put 300ml water in a pan, add the butter and bring to the boil. Add salt to the water and then the cabbage. The cabbage is ready when it is nice and green and still has a bite.

Turn out the pies and serve with a scoop of mashed potato and the strained buttered greens. Pour over the reserved gravy and enjoy.

# CHAPTER TWO

# A Business Opportunity

**IT WOULD NOT BE INCORRECT TO SAY** that without the involvement of John Fuller the site where Thomas Urlin, William Mawson and the Thompson brothers brewed their beers would be a very different space today. For a start, given the financial problems prior to the enlistment of Fuller, brewing would have probably ground to a halt sometime in the early 1830s, with perhaps a rival concern snapping up the business and then eventually closing it.

If we want to speculate further, the chances are that it would have fallen prey to the neighbouring Lamb Brewery, whose early 20th-century tower can still be seen from the passing A4. However, none of this happened. Fuller was the white knight, the saviour, the firm hand on the tiller that steered what would eventually become Fuller, Smith & Turner into calmer waters.

First of all, let's travel down through the centuries and try to understand him. We know he was born in 1765 and became the protégé of a wealthy distant cousin, a financier and moneylender named Gerard Dutton Fleetwood. Fuller and his wife also seem to have lived with Fleetwood in his home in Leatherhead. When Fleetwood died in 1795, Fuller was the sole heir to his entire fortune – and his 'loan book'. In 1790, he'd also purchased the estate of Neston Park, near Corsham in Wiltshire, and built Neston House; the estate has been the family seat ever since. A portrait, painted perhaps when he was in his late twenties, suggests a quiet man, calm and thoughtful, though clearly aware of the fashions of the late 18th century. He doesn't have a wig (they were falling out of favour) and his hair is cut short in what was then dubbed a 'Roman' style; the collar

of the top of his dark coat is up, while a high-necked white cravat completes the picture. It all hints at a country gentleman who is not unfamiliar with travelling up to 'town', as London was (and still is) called.

According to director Richard Fuller, 'I think he picked up information about the brewery even though he didn't know anything about brewing. Presumably someone told him that there was a brewery that was recoverable and could do with investment and he went in with the Thompson brothers.'

Given the acumen and foresight with which he developed the brewery in the next few years, we can imagine that a steely-eyed determination and robust approach towards business were also among his attributes.

This drive to success is all the more remarkable for the fact that, when Philip Wood's offer of a partnership arrived on the Neston Park breakfast table, Fuller was already in his mid-sixties; this was in an era when the life expectancy for men was in the forties. But he rose to the challenge, and most likely also considered that here was a fine opportunity to invest money on behalf of his son, John Bird Fuller.

**AT THE TIME,** beer was still the national drink, consumed at all times of the day and at various strengths (though tea was also popular with all classes). The brewing industry in Britain continued to be dominated by porter, especially in London, where monstrous vats held tens of thousands of gallons of beer (sometimes these vats, as happened in Tottenham Court Road, London, in 1814, would burst with catastrophic results). The Industrial Revolution was

NESTON HOUSE, WHICH WAS BUILT BY JOHN FULLER AFTER PURCHASING THE ESTATE IN 1790

changing the country and the brewing industry was not immune to the technological advances.

In 1817, for instance, Daniel Wheeler created an apparatus to roast malt at a high temperature without charring it – this was called the 'New or Improved Method of Drying and Preparing Malt' and produced what came to be called black malt, an essential part of the grain bill for dark beers. Then there was the saccharometer (also known as the hydrometer), which, although it had been around since the end of the 18th century, was starting to become popular with brewers, as it enabled them to determine the strength and consistency of their beers more accurately than before. It wouldn't be hard to imagine that, when Fuller got the opportunity to invest, he would have been aware of developments like these.

It has also been thought in the past that Fuller was perhaps inspired to become financially involved because of a family connection, albeit a tenuous one, with the Chiswick neighbourhood. This presumed link was the affable clergyman and historian Dr Thomas Fuller, who had been rector of the nearby village of Cranford from 1658 until his death in 1661. Dr Fuller had a powerful reputation as a preacher, and a rather lesser one as the writer

of innumerable poems, satires, pamphlets and histories, though it is said that he was one of the first writers to make a living from his own words. The best known of these was his *History of the Worthies of England*, a series of the lives of notable Englishmen, which displays much wit and learning, as well as a lamentable fondness for puns. He even suggested his own epitaph: Fuller's Earth. But perhaps the doctor's most fitting memorial is the description of him by Charles Lamb as a 'dear, fine, silly, old angel'. However, delicious as the connection might be, according to Richard Fuller, 'We are not 100 per cent convinced about the link with Thomas Fuller.'

John Fuller seized the business opportunity offered by Wood and within a few years had stamped his authority on the affairs of the brewery, even though he rarely visited it. For a start, the original, equal partnership of Thompson, Wood and Fuller, established in 1829, was a short-lived one. Henry Thompson sold his share in the company, squandered the capital and was declared bankrupt in 1831. Philip Wood died in 1832 (and it soon became clear that he too had been bankrupt). Fuller bought his share, thus becoming a major shareholder, with two-thirds of the total.

JOHN FULLER IN HIS YOUTH

# CHANGING TASTES OF THE 18TH & 19TH CENTURIES

PORTER REMAINED KING, though the sour, aged porters of the 18th century were giving way to milder, fresher versions, which were served as a mixture of old and new beer. Another popular beer in London in the early part of the 19th century was 'half and half', a mixture of ale and porter. The drink of the working classes was mild ale, a beer that was young and therefore hadn't taken on some of the sharp, acidic notes of a 'stale' beer. Further up the social ladder, we find middle-class drinkers plumping for pale ales, including India pale ales. Hock, a name that had been in use in Fuller's since the 18th century, was an Old English word for harvest, and was applied to harvest ales.

However, the brewery's finances were still distinctly rocky. Beer sales had slumped in 1831, causing a loss of over £3,000 for the year. The previous year had seen the passing of the Beer Act, where beer duty was abolished and every householder was given the right to sell beer provided they paid for a two-guinea licence from the Excise. This had led to a massive growth in beer houses, which also meant a growth in outlets for breweries to sell their beers – evidently the brewery wasn't in a position to prosper from this.

There were other financial concerns on the horizon. The remaining Thompson, Douglas, was in a parlous financial state. He already owed the company £14,000, and was about to become liable for his brother's equally massive debts. Ever the businessman, Fuller now tightened his grip by allowing Douglas to borrow further from the business, using his third share as a mortgage.

ON 5 JANUARY 1832, Fuller and Thompson signed their new articles of partnership, which were intended to last for 18 years. This proved to be hopelessly optimistic. The articles defined Douglas as 'the resident and acting partner', who was to 'devote the whole of his time and energy to the business', while John Fuller spent most of his time in Wiltshire. It was very soon clear that Douglas Thompson was not so much a partner as an albatross around Fuller's neck. He seemed weak, feckless and muddle-headed, and it was also said he was 'under the thumb' of his second wife.

Fuller was well aware of Douglas' shortcomings. To safeguard his own interests and to keep a close eye on affairs in Chiswick, he hired an accountant named J.W. Smith. Smith was to visit the brewery once a week and compile a report on purchases, sales and beer production, which he would then send down to Neston.

According to contemporary reports, Smith could have walked straight out of the pages of Dickens. He was a dour and humourless middle-aged man, devoted to his job and meticulous in his paperwork: in short, the very antithesis of Douglas Thompson's casual approach. Smith was also inordinately proud of his position as auditor to the Carlton, Athenaeum and Travellers Clubs, and made regular appearances in the Chancery courts. Plunging into the scruffy, deceitful, extravagant world of the Thompson family could hardly have made for a starker contrast.

There was another Dickensian personality slinking around the brewery, but he has only come down to us by his nickname of Slee (a word that is apparently derived from Middle English, meaning sly and cunning, which seems rather apt). Whatever his true name, Slee caused Smith no end of trouble. He had been originally hired by Wood and Thompson to run a newly built spirit store at the brewery, which could be argued wasn't the wisest of moves given that Slee was at the time in France, where he had fled to escape prosecution by the Excise. In his absence, his house in Brighton was searched and 'some most extraordinary contrivance for smuggling and cheating the government' was found. A less suitable person to take charge of a spirit store would be hard to imagine.

Nevertheless, despite his troubles with the law Slee in due course arrived to take up his new post. We can imagine that the punctilious Smith took a deep dislike to the man – he certainly watched him closely if his regular reports to his employer were any indication. Slee, he disclosed, was in the habit of visiting public houses and making ridiculous promises about supplies to the tenants. Worse still, 'his conduct at Chiswick has been most disreputable: he has seduced and has been living openly with one of Mr Thompson's maids, who was at last turned out of Slee's house by his own daughter'. There were also tales of nepotism: it was reported that Slee gave jobs in the stores to brothers of 'the woman whom he had debauched'. Something had to be done and in June 1834 the spirit store was closed down and Slee dismissed. Sly to the last, the rogue managed to sneak away with two dozen bottles of unsold wine from the cellar.

The letters that passed between John Fuller and J.W. Smith were full of exasperation with the ineptness of Thompson. 'My opinion,' wrote Fuller late in 1834, 'is that the whole family possesses very much the same principles, that is they care not as to any matter of right whose property they get into their hands to lavish away. The Brewery business is going on flour-ishingly but we must not expect all sunshine and fair weather. I know the great risk and hazard I have taken on myself...'

However, inept as he was we must feel some sympathy for Thompson when news came of his eldest son's demise in Australia. The luckless lad had under-standably turned his back on the family business and gone to live in Western Australia, where he had been granted an area of land. In 1835, he was drowned when his boat sank in the Swan river – an echo of the fate of old Captain Byrne. Douglas only heard of the tragedy a year later when reading about it in a newspaper. Doubtless he was shocked and mourned his son's death, but it didn't stop him from writing to the governor in Perth, claiming his son's land. The lad, he said, 'had received from me altogether £1,500 to £1,700. A sum which then I could ill spare owing to the unfortunate circumstances in which I had been placed by the ill management of his uncle... Upon the winning

## TAKING ROOT

IN 1816, HEAVY RAIN and cool temperatures devastated harvests worldwide and caused food shortages; it has gone down in history as the 'year without a summer'. This global cooling was the result of a massive volcanic eruption in the Far East, with the resulting dust and detritus from the explosion being pushed high into the atmosphere and circling the world. This was another blow to Europe, coming as it did just after the end of the Napoleonic Wars in 1815. Famine stalked the continent, while food riots erupted in the United Kingdom. We don't know how the brewery coped with such calamities but it cannot have been easy selling beer at this time. However, there was a brighter side to the year, when samples of a wisteria plant were brought into the country from China. One of them went to Kew Gardens, while the other was planted at the brewery outside what was then one of the brewers' cottages (it now houses offices). The one at Kew died and a cutting from Chiswick had to be sent over to resurrect it, but the plant at the brewery flourished and has done ever since, making it the oldest wisteria in the United Kingdom.

of the concern I found myself the loser to the amount of at least £20,000. In fact I am absolutely beginning again.' Despite several years of campaigning, the claim came to nothing.

IN MARCH 1839, John Fuller suffered a severe attack of influenza and died aged 74. His estates were inherited by his son, John Bird Fuller, as were his financial problems. Brewery profits were falling sharply and the new decade would come to be known as the Hungry Forties. This was a period when many poor people could scarcely afford bread, let alone beer, consumption of which had fallen from an annual 33 gallons per capita in 1800 to 19 during the 1840s.

Alongside these problems, Douglas Thompson had landed the brewery in a fresh crisis. After the death of his second wife, he wasn't a widower for long and this time married a widow with seven children. Once again we find Smith's moral antennae quivering with alarm, as he noted that the third Mrs Thompson was 'the daughter of our maltster Muggeridge', and that the match was 'a result of a deep laid scheme to supply the brewery with malt and hops as the sole supplier'. However, what really shocked was that, under the existing deed of partnership, provision had to be made for all Thompson's dependants in the event of his death. The number of dependants had now swollen to over a dozen. Such a liability, added to Douglas' still outstanding debts, was too much to bear and would totally cripple the company.

John Bird Fuller now displayed a steeliness and decisiveness that would stand him and future generations in good stead whenever faced with a crisis. In January 1841, he informed Douglas that their partnership was to be dissolved within 12 months and that the faithful J.W. Smith would become manager in his place. Douglas was also told that if he relinquished his share in the business, he would be paid an allowance of £400 a year (roughly £34,000 in today's money). These were pretty generous terms, but Thompson squealed loudly that no provision had been made for his large family. The iron resolve of Fuller was not to be weakened and he tightened the screw by withdrawing Thompson's right to draw cheques. This forced surrender, and the

THE BREWERY CIRCA 1845, AT THE DAWN OF THE FOUNDATION OF FULLER, SMITH & TURNER

# BACKGROUND TO THE BREWING INDUSTRY IN THE FIRST PART OF THE 19TH CENTURY

THE PORTER BREWERIES STILL DOMINATED the London brewing industry at the start of the 19th century – of 98 common brewers in London in 1815, the 12 main porter brewers were responsible for 75 per cent of beer made in the capital. Outside London, the number of common brewers was on the increase – the figure grew from 1,787 to 2,791 in the years between 1824 and 1839. Private brewing, on the other hand, was in decline, presumably because it was becoming less economic to brew at home. The status of brewers also became more socially acceptable – some, like Samuel Whitbread, sat as MPs and many had substantial country estates. It was said that in rural England if a young man of a 'well-to-do' family failed to enter the army or learn a profession, brewing was one of the careers to be pursued. However, the spectre of temperance was starting to haunt the industry and would be a constant challenge throughout the rest of the century.

deed of dissolution took effect from January 1842. Like limpets clinging to a rock, the Thompson family could not be dislodged that easily. The disgraced Henry made a pathetic reappearance, offering his services as manager, and blaming past disasters on his brother and the long-dead Philip Wood. This was very much the action of a desperate man, for he died a month later. Douglas, meanwhile, having been evicted from the brewery, departed the country for Calais, leaving both his family and finances in chaos behind him. Fuller might have been a resolute businessman, but he also felt some sympathy for the abandoned family and arranged support for the wife and children. Gradually, the Thompson nightmare faded.

AS THERE IS AFTER A GREAT STORM has passed, so there was much work to be done to rebuild the business. Fuller's job was to convince the brewing industry and, indeed, the business world at large, that for the first time in 35 years an honest man was in control of the Chiswick premises. Aided by J.W. Smith, he began to restore the brewery's reputation. How gratified Smith must have been when the company received a glowing letter from William Gutteridge, a local estate agent. Gutteridge wrote: 'The gentle-manly and businesslike manner in which you appear

as manager of the Chiswick Brewery not only reminds me of old times, but also in my idea reflects great credit upon the principal of that Establishment, particularly after the treatment I have experienced from the original name.'

Despite this encouragement, John Bird Fuller was very aware that his own resources were not enough to bring the brewery back to full health. Therefore, he started looking about for new investors. We don't know how they met but the link in the chain that would lead to today's successful brewery was John Smith, a wealthy partner of Edward Ind at the Romford brewery in Essex. Smith had joined in 1816, when Ind's previous business partner retired. The brewery was very successful and Smith was responsible for patenting an automatic weighing machine for malt. However, Fuller persuaded John Smith to sever his ties with Ind and transfer his money from Romford to Chiswick in 1845. This move, incidentally, did no harm to Ind's career; he was joined by the brothers Coope and began trading under the name of Ind and Coope, also opening a brewery in Burton-on-Trent in 1856 to produce Burton-style pale ales. It seemed like an amicable separation – agreement was made between the two ex-partners that Ind Coope would only trade to the east of the Aldgate Pump and Fuller's to the west.

John Smith did not arrive alone. His investment in Fuller's brewery was made in the names of his son Henry Smith and son-in-law John Turner, who was also the head brewer at Romford. However, the actual process of drawing up the articles of partnership was agonisingly slow, which was apparently due largely to the endeavours (or lack of) of another individual who sounds like a character from a Dickens novel, though slightly less sinister than Slee.

The lawyer the future partners had engaged was a Mr Frere of Lincoln's Inn, apparently an ageing and slothful character, whose snail-like progress infuriated Fuller, who had a dislike of what he called 'dilly-dallying'. Come the middle of summer in 1845 things had scarcely moved and John Smith visited J.W. Smith at Chiswick, expressing concern at the continuing delay, which he warned could lose the brewery at least £1,000 a year in trade. J.W. Smith

only in his early thirties, was proving to be just as tough and determined in bargaining as John Bird Fuller. Fuller, eager to expedite matters, declared that he must be allowed to appoint an agent to look after his affairs at the brewery. Smith lodged a strong objection. When the more easy-going John Turner complained mildly at the delay in letting him occupy the brewer's house, Smith argued his case. Smith senior, meanwhile, was losing enthusiasm for the affair and threatening to withdraw his money.

J.W. Smith was caught in the middle of these increasingly testy exchanges and it must have been a stressful time for him. Not only would he have been aware that the prospect of the union could deprive him of his old position, but he also had to act as go-between for the warring factions, without provoking John Smith or J.B. Fuller. Somehow, he maintained a delicate balancing act worthy of the most adept tightrope walker. J.W. Smith succeeded in flattering his employer and encouraging Smith and Turner at the same time, while also badgering the lethargic Frere and fighting to keep his own place.

'Messrs Smith and Turner have both declared that they do not see how they can get on without my assistance,' he wrote to Frere. 'It cannot be expected that while I have any connection with the Brewery I should be content to sink into insignificance.'

**A NEW YEAR DAWNED** and the main actors in what was turning out to be a long-running saga must have hoped that things could be resolved. But no: Frere was still deaf to all exhortations and this time he took to his bed with gout and bronchitis, followed by a long period of convalescence. The months passed and a grim silence fell upon the parties concerned. It was only by pleading old age that John Smith was at last able to goad the solicitor into action. The articles of partnership were finally signed on 19 November 1846.

Under the terms of the deed, Fuller retained one-half of the total shares in the company, while Henry Smith

passed on this warning to Frere and suggested an immediate meeting, so that matters could be hurried along. Unsurprisingly, this was felt to be too hasty for Mr Frere, who replied by messenger that he 'would not be in town for a few days'.

The waiting game continued and the uncertainty heightened the tension between the prospective partners; matters could so easily go wrong. Henry Smith, though

# INGREDIENTS FOR BREWING
# YEAST

**YEAST IS THE MAGICAL INGREDIENT** that turns the sugars in what is called the hopped wort into alcohol and carbon dioxide. After the boil, the hopped wort is cooled and pumped into fermenting vessels. Yeast is then introduced into the equation and fermentation begins. Before the action of yeast was explained by Louis Pasteur, among others, fermentation was a mystery and often called 'goddisgoode' by brewers, who turned to the Almighty when they couldn't work out how they ended up with such a potent brew. Fuller's has two strains of yeast on site – their own and Gales. They are stored at opposite ends of the brewery to avoid any potential cross-contamination. Fuller's yeast gives orange citrus and toffee flavours to the beer (marmalade notes can be discernible at higher alcoholic strengths), whereas Gales yeast tends to bring a soft fruit flavour to the fermentations, with red berry fruits coming through. Both strains are stored off site, kept under liquid nitrogen and cannot be shared with any other brewer.

and John Turner took one-quarter each, for which they paid £31,000. They were termed 'active resident partners', occupying the 'manager's house and the outbuildings and gardens thereto situated at Chiswick, except ONE room', which was to be reserved for Fuller's use. J.W. Smith, as he had feared, ceased to be manager but was retained as an accountant; however, his salary was reduced from £700 to £300 as a result.

As well as finances, Henry Smith and John Turner brought with them a welcome bonus in the shape of an extensive list of private customers. For these, a special type of beer had to be brewed. It was known as 'table beer', which was a beer low in alcohol and, as its name suggests, was intended to be drunk at the dinner table.

This was quite a change for the brewery, which seems to have been remarkably conservative in its range of beers until then. Under the Thompsons, only two

Marlow, who was the reliable and efficient head brewer, had died in 1845 and his replacement turned out to be a bungler. John Bird Fuller knew absolutely nothing about the brewing process, and must have been very relieved when Turner took over. In 1850, Turner's son John E. Turner, nicknamed John Jr, came of age and was appointed head brewer at a salary of £100 a year. He held this position until his death in 1884, but never became a partner.

NOW, AT LAST, the fortunes of the brewery entered a more tranquil period. One of the later Fullers, Dillwyn Fleetwood, made a series of notes on this period. He wrote: 'During all these years the business continued to flourish; taxation was light; there was no beer duty. Employment, in the neighbourhood, at any rate, was good; therefore there was plenty of money to spend on beer, which was both strong and cheap. Whether it was also uniformly good is

## DID YOU KNOW...

*Beer is the third most popular drink in the world.*
*Tea is number two and water number one.*

kinds had ever been brewed: ale, which sold at 54 shillings a barrel (which held 36 gallons), and hock, at 33 shillings. Porter, which had soared in popularity since the 1740s, had not originally been produced on the premises, but bought in from other brewers. It was only in 1841 that porter brewing began at the Griffin – just when it was going into terminal decline as a national drink. This was also the time of the growing ascendancy of pale ale, influenced by the brisk, hoppy beers coming out of Burton-on-Trent. This variety of beer was helped by the removal of the glass tax in 1845, which meant that these beers were served in clear glasses (instead of the old pewter mugs), with drinkers perhaps being more receptive to a glass that showed off the golden clarity of their beer rather than the murk of porter.

A further and much-needed lift to the technical side of the business came with John Turner's arrival. Thomas

rather more than doubtful. However that may have been, the Private Trade, after making a modest start in 1846 with 3,433 barrels and gross receipts at £4,298 (while the gross receipts from the Publican Trade were £40,570), increased steadily until in 1866 it shows gross receipts of £46,081 against the Public Trade's £45,543.'

After the tumultuous times of the past few years, the new dynasty of Fuller, Smith & Turner had evidently brought stability and profitability to the business. New challenges lay ahead, new innovations, new modes of doing business, but for the moment the three families could allow themselves a brief moment of congratulation and possibly celebrate with a glass of Fuller, Smith & Turner's finest.

# TASTING NOTE
## 1845, 6.3%

SOME 150 YEARS AFTER FULLER, SMITH AND TURNER decided to join forces, the brewery's then head brewer, Reg Drury, produced this superlative celebratory beer, which took its inspiration from a beer brewed by Fuller's in the middle of the 19th century. This nod to history and heritage was accentuated by the use of amber malt in the recipe, which was popular in the 19th century. Another ingredient with its origins in the same period is the sole hop used, Goldings. The beer is matured for 100 days, and also bottle-conditioned, with the brewery recommending that it has a shelf life of two years; it was originally only meant to be brewed as a one-off but is now a regular and even occasionally appears in cask.

Copper-chestnut in colour, it sits beneath a firm espresso crema head; nuts, raisins, coffee and a dairy/milky-like note emerge on the nose plus a ringing chime of fruitiness, perhaps ripe red plums or even orange marmalade. On the palate it's chewy and spirituous, is fortified by more fruitiness and has a chocolatey smoothness in the middle before finishing off dry and cracker-like with the whisper of a juicy fruitiness. A big beer.

# Vintage Ale Sticky Toffee Pudding with Salted Caramel Ice Cream and Toffee Sauce

Serves 8

## INGREDIENTS

**For the sticky toffee pudding:**

| | |
|---|---|
| 400g | dates, stoned and chopped |
| 600ml | Fuller's Vintage Ale |
| 150g | unsalted butter, diced, at room temperature |
| 350g | soft dark brown sugar |
| 6 tbsp | golden syrup |
| 6 | eggs |
| 400g | self-raising flour |
| 4 tsp | bicarbonate of soda |

**For the crumble topping:**

| | |
|---|---|
| 130g | caster sugar |
| 130g | plain flour |
| 2 tsp | cornflour |
| 120g | unsalted butter |

**For the toffee sauce:**

| | |
|---|---|
| 600ml | double cream |
| 100g | butter |
| 250g | soft dark brown sugar |
| 3 tbsp | golden syrup |
| 100ml | Fuller's Vintage Ale |

**To serve:**

salted caramel ice cream

## METHOD

To make the sticky toffee pudding, preheat the oven to 180°C/fan oven 160°C/gas mark 4 and line a 20cm square tin with greaseproof paper. Put the chopped dates and ale into a saucepan. Bring to the boil and simmer for 3 minutes, then leave to cool. Next, in a mixer, cream the butter and sugar together. Add the syrup and whisk in well. Add the eggs one by one, whisking well after each addition. Sift the flour into the batter in two parts and fold in gently. Add the bicarbonate of soda to the dates and mix well. Fold the dates into the batter, pour into the prepared tin and put in the oven immediately. Bake for approximately 20–25 minutes, until a skewer inserted in the centre comes out clean. Allow to cool in the tin before turning out and cutting into squares or oblongs.

The crumble adds texture but is used mainly to prevent the ice cream from melting. Preheat the oven to 160°C/fan oven 140°C/gas mark 3 and line a baking tray with greaseproof paper. Place the caster sugar, plain flour and cornflour in a bowl. Melt the butter and add this to the dry ingredients, mixing together well. Place the mixture on to the prepared tray and bake in the oven for 6 minutes, then take out and mix around with a fork and return to the oven for a further 6 minutes. Take out, mix around again and allow to cool.

Prepare the toffee sauce by placing all the ingredients (except the ale) in a saucepan. Bring to the boil and simmer for 2–3 minutes. Add the ale and bring back to the boil, then simmer for a further 5–6 minutes until the alcohol has cooked off and the mixture has a sauce consistency. Allow to cool slightly before using.

If necessary, warm up the sauce in a small pan and pour into a serving jug. Heat the sticky toffee pudding either in the oven or the microwave and serve sprinkled with a little of the crumble and a scoop of salted caramel ice cream on top. Drizzle with warm toffee sauce.

# CHAPTER THREE

# Growing Pains

**THE SECOND HALF OF THE 19TH CENTURY** was a time of growth for Fuller, Smith & Turner, a company that to the outside world had all the appearance of being a comfortable family firm. Members of all three families were involved in the business and the number of pubs owned continued to increase. According to Gillian Wheeler in the privately published *A Brewery and its environment – the Griffin Brewery in Chiswick 1840–1870* (1975):

> ... in the 1840s there were twenty three public houses in Chiswick of which twelve belonged to the Griffin Brewery. They also owned:-

| | |
|---|---|
| 20 in Brentford | 13 in Hammersmith |
| 6 in Ealing | 5 in Acton |
| 3 in Hounslow | 2 in Hayes. |

The writer also made the point that in the same decade the brewery had further pubs in Parsons Green, Hanger Lane and Knightsbridge. This wide circle of trading obviously needed a decent-sized workforce and in the 1851 census we discover that the brewery consisted of:

| | |
|---|---|
| John Turner | Brewer, employing 33 men |
| Liza Turner | |
| John E. Turner | Son, clerk |
| Elizabeth Turner | Daughter |
| Jemima Turner | Daughter, scholar |
| Mary Turner | Daughter, scholar at house |
| Henry Smith | Brewer |
| Mary Walker | Servant |

Interestingly enough, John Bird Fuller does not appear on the roster. Presumably he remained at Neston, but still managed to keep an eye on matters.

The next census, in 1861, did not illustrate the number of people employed at the brewery, but Wheeler believes that it would be fair to assume that the number would have increased.

However, amid all these positive signs of growth, there was, as was the custom with all family firms, one incurably weak link – the question of succession. Partners grew old or died and their successors were nominated: some were assets to the company; some definitely not; while others were simply not interested. This uncertainty preyed on the minds of the three families and periodically erupted into squabbles over the next half-century.

**THE FIRST OF THESE DISPUTES** bubbled up as early as 1851. Henry Smith, though heading into middle age, was still a bachelor living with the Turners on site at the brewery. Now it emerged that he was having an 'affair with his fancy', as one of the partners put it, and the 'fancy' had a disgruntled husband.

Despite being essentially a private matter, this revelation was the cause of great consternation at the brewery. John Smith, every inch the stern Victorian father, expressed his outrage by threatening to withdraw his money (and thus Henry's quarter share) from the business. John Turner sprang to the son's defence with some characteristically blunt language. The only one left to make the peace was John Bird Fuller.

He summoned Henry Smith to Neston and persuaded him to write two letters: one to the lady, which ended the liaison, and the other to his father, offering an apology. 'I can scarcely think,' Fuller confided to his accountant, 'Mr John Smith intends to take such strong measures of withdrawing his money throwing as it were his son out of bread.'

But John Smith seems to have been a difficult man to mollify. He would not be swayed by the pleadings of his partners or by his son: the future of the enterprise looked bleak. You can imagine that, with a heavy heart and perhaps recalling the tempestuous times before 1845, Fuller prepared to dissolve the partnership and buy out Henry's share himself.

Then, as if it were a play of the Victorian stage, where with one bound the hero (usually called Jack and a more manly hero you could never find) was free, the episode came to a satisfactory close, though there are

no surviving sources to tell us how. Evidently Smith relented, forgave his son and continued on with the original arrangement.

As for Henry, perhaps chastened by his intemperate lifestyle and cowed by the moral strictures of the time, he seems to have turned into a model citizen in later years (though he never married and, as far as is known, never got involved in any further untoward romantic tangles). According to Richard Fuller, 'After getting into an awful mess because he behaved inappropriately with a married woman, it seems that as a penance he devoted the last part of his life and career to becoming a prominent benefactor of St Nicholas Church.' According to a plaque in the church, he became churchwarden there.

He also served as a Chiswick Improvement Commissioner from 1858. This was a body of community-minded men, which included John

BRINGING GROWTH TO CHISWICK: TURNHAM GREEN UNDERGROUND STATION IN THE 19TH CENTURY

Turner, responsible for overseeing the upkeep of the local sewers, drains and roads, and for maintaining a wharf on the Thames. This, after all, was an era when Chiswick was growing rapidly; given that its population doubled between 1841 and 1861, such improvements were vital to the area's health. At the time the main street of Chiswick ran up from the river, past St Nicholas Church on the left and the Griffin Brewery and Sich & Co on the right. In the 1831 census, Chiswick had a population of 4,994; this grew to 15,663 in 1881, possibly as a consequence of the 1869 opening of the Turnham Green underground station. This enabled people to work in central London then return home in the evening and perhaps enjoy a glass of Fuller's beer as a reward for a hard day's graft.

AS THE 1850S TICKED ON BY we can imagine that John Bird Fuller was looking forward to the future with confidence. There was, at any rate, no problem about who was to succeed him. His eldest son, John Augustus, was serving with the British Army in the Crimean War, but fully intended to take on his father's role at the brewery in due course. His second son, George Pargiter, had just finished at Oxford. 'There are not to be found two more prudent and well-disposed young men,' wrote Fuller proudly.

Meanwhile, more of the past was vanishing. In 1856, there appeared in Fuller's private ledger the entry: 'J.W. Smith died – regrettably'. Rarely can so faithful a servant have been given so offhanded an epitaph, but we should not judge the early Victorian sensibilities too harshly. This was an age of quietness, a time of hiding emotions, the beginning of the stiff upper lip.

A link with the past had thus been broken and within a few years a link with the future was tragically gone too. John Augustus had remained in the army, and was by 1859 stationed in Gibraltar. News was scarce but, as far as the family knew, he had either been wounded or fallen ill (they didn't know at the time but he was suffering from wounds sustained during the Crimean War). In September of that year, John Bird Fuller received a poignant letter, which was the last he would get from his eldest son.

PLAQUE REMEMBERING HENRY SMITH IN ST NICHOLAS CHURCH

This morning I brought up a good quantity of blood from my chest and I now begin to think it possible that my present illness may turn out fatal... I wish it had been permitted me to see dear old Neston once more and I am afraid that the news of my death will come upon you all with dreadful suddenness.

By the time John Bird read these words his son was already dead. In his grief the old man turned to his other son, George Pargiter, pinning all his hopes on him. Now was the moment for him to begin his training at the brewery (he had been drawing a salary of £150 a year since 1856) and prepare to take command.

Outside the human tragedies, business continued to expand and a considerable amount of building was carried out. Between 1855 and 1863 a new storeroom and two new tun rooms were completed. Turnover rose and with the expiration of the first deed of partnership looming in 1866, Smith and Turner began

# GEORGE PARGITER FULLER 1833-1927

OF THE THREE FAMILIES that made up the brewery, if there is one member who was perhaps most influential during his life, then that is 'GP'. Technological advances in brewing were noted and acted on, while he also had time to sit as a Liberal MP for ten years. His middle name Pargiter came from the Pargiter family of London, into which John Fuller married in the late 18th century. He was a keen cricketer and represented the Oxford University Cricket Club in two 'varsity' matches, in 1854 and 1855. When he died in 1927, his *Times* obituary noted that he 'was known as "the Grand Old Man" of Wiltshire'.

pressing Fuller for a bigger slice of the cake. They pointed out that since they had arrived, the average annual profits had risen from just over £6,000 to more than £16,000. Nearly all the outstanding mortgages had been paid off, and many new properties had been purchased. In view of this they demanded that they should be made co-equal partners with Fuller, each owning a third share.

John Bird refused even to entertain the idea. He told Smith and Turner that they could either renew the existing terms of the partnership or be bought out. His only compromise was to offer the pair an increase in their salaries for managing the brewery.

The three men had once again reached what Fuller called a 'deplorable deadlock'. The only way out of it was to ask for an independent opinion from a barrister. Counsel George Markham Gifford pondered the conflicting claims and solemnly declared that if the parties could not concur, the whole brewery

would have to be sold by private auction to the highest bidder. This bombshell seemingly brought everyone to their senses. Fuller, Smith and Turner managed to patch up their differences for on 1 May 1866 they all signed the new deed of partnership. The proportion of the shares – and most other clauses – remained as before. The one vital alteration was that Smith and Turner were to be paid a percentage commission on sales to the private trade. Apparently, this was satisfactory.

Another period of comparative tranquillity followed this storm. The company ledgers give a picture of steady growth and improvement. During 1866, a new stable and a store beneath the garden were built. The brewery owned over £12,000 worth of 'cooperage, Firkins and Kilderkins' – a firkin was a nine-gallon cask, its name thought to be derived from the Middle Dutch *vierdekijnm*, which meant the fourth part of a barrel; a kilderkin was twice its volume and again its name came from Middle Dutch. This was a sure sign of a healthy trading position, as was the 'horses account' of £4,901, which showed a stock of 36.

As has been shown, Chiswick in the middle of the 19th century was a relatively peaceful community, beyond the bounds of Hammersmith, still showing signs of its rural past (after all, Hogarth's House, which is close by on the A4, was his country retreat). But it was beginning to expand rapidly. The brewery itself was in what was called Old Chiswick. There was a growing residential area along the Chiswick Mall, which ran parallel to the river, with smaller properties going up along Chiswick Lane and Devonshire Road. The rate books showed that many brewery employees lived in the vicinity, though not all of them worked for Fuller, Smith & Turner. The Griffin Brewery had a close rival right on its doorstep. This was the Lamb Brewery, owned by the Sich family and boasting, for many years, a workforce as big as its neighbour's.

MEANWHILE, THE MAN who had forged the partnership between the three families, and provided the iron link when matters looked unstable, died: 27 May 1872 was the day when John Bird Fuller relinquished his earthly duties. For nearly 40 years, a man who had been described by his contemporaries and colleagues as honest, courteous and unyielding had held the company together. His successor was to be an altogether larger and more imaginative personality – his son, George Pargiter Fuller, who inherited his half share.

George Pargiter Fuller (or 'GP', as he was known and still is by his descendants) can be described as perhaps the most formidable figure in the history of Fuller's, firmly gripping the helm for over half a century. He is also one of the most interesting. As a brewery owner, he encouraged several new enterprises, such as the maltings, and sanctioned the latest technology and processes – this period of the 19th century saw brewing become engulfed by technological advances, including the ability to control the temperature during a brew, which then led to all-year-round brewing. Then there was the work of Louis Pasteur, which uncovered a greater understanding of what yeast did during

# SICH & CO, LAMB BREWERY, CHURCH STREET

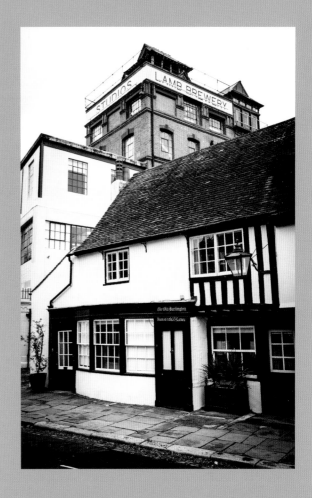

**TRAVELLERS PASSING FULLER'S ALONG THE A4** might be forgiven for thinking that the tower brewery building to the right is also part of the same complex. This is what remains of the former Lamb Brewery, which from the late 18th century was a near neighbour. Owned by the Sich family, it possessed its own estate of pubs, including the Lamb and the Burlington Arms (both closed as pubs in the 1920s), but in 1921 it was taken over by Watney, Combe, Reid. Fuller's then bought the building and brewing came to an end, though the company sold it on later and it is now private flats.

# INGREDIENTS FOR BREWING
# SUSTAINABILITY

**ALL BREWERIES HAVE A DUTY TO RECYCLE** their used raw materials. Fuller's is no different, which is why every day you will see a large lorry in the brewery's yard being filled with spent grains. This is then taken away and used as animal feed for cattle and spent yeast, as well as going into making Marmite, is also fed to pigs. This is nothing new for the brewery: back in the 19th century the brewery's stock of horse manure was sold for £45 per cartload. In summer, the horses grazed in the adjoining Homefields alongside the prens where the brewery's pigs grew fat on spent barley. Sometimes it's best to keep to the old ways.

fermentation. A variety of technological brewing aids were developed, many of which would be on show at the annual Brewers' National Exhibition and Market, which started to be held at the Royal Agricultural Hall in Islington from 1879.

As a farmer, Fuller eagerly embraced modern methods, buying one of the earliest steam-powered hay driers and building his own automatic stock feeder, which was controlled by the mechanism from a grandfather clock! As a major landowner, he considerably expanded the house at Neston Park, and installed an electric generator and windmills for raising water. As a public figure, he was stoutly Liberal, serving as MP for Westbury from 1885 to 1895, and is reputed to have turned down a peerage. As a family man, he ensured a solid future by fathering five sons (and mapping out their careers) and a daughter.

According to Richard Fuller, 'There is a strong entrepreneurial streak in the Fullers. What GP did was that he loaned money to all his sons and encouraged them to set up their own businesses. One son ran Neston, another worked at the brewery, another the Avon Rubber Company and the youngest son had a tea plantation and rubber in what was then called Ceylon.'

His long reign began serenely enough. Indeed, the records contain no major crises – even with the signing of the third deed of partnership in 1887. For this portentous event, a fresh inventory and valuation was drawn up. It is an illuminating document, especially when compared with the 'rest' prepared a century earlier.

Extracts describing the brewery premises shine a light on his inheritance:

> On the right of the Entrance Yard, the Counting House, Strong Room and Offices. The private Residence occupied by Mr Henry Smith. A building of three floors adjoining. Ground Floor forming Kitchen etc, with Hop and Sugar Stores over — the Roof formed by the iron Cold Liquor Back.
> The Brewhouse, in which are the Mash Tuns, Coppers and other brewing plants.
> The Malt Loft and Cellar under Working Tun Rooms and Cleansing Rooms with Carpenters' Shop and storerooms over one Beer Store.
> Engine House, Boiler House, Vat House.
> Timekeeper's office and Allowance Store.
> Settling Back Room and Fining Store.
> Another Boiler House. Cask Shed.

THE NEXT GENERATION: *(LEFT TO RIGHT)* EDWARD TREVELYAN TURNER, FRANK SMITH AND WILLIAM FULLER IN 1887

GRIFFIN BREWERY CC AT HOMEFIELDS, 1886. FRANK SMITH (BOWLER HAT) IS SECOND FROM THE RIGHT IN THE BACK ROW. WILLIAM FULLER IS IN THE CENTRE OF THE MIDDLE ROW, WITH 'TREVY' TURNER (STRIPED TIE) AND R.F.L. TURNER ON HIS LEFT

Cask Steaming Shed with Boiler and Engine House at the end.

A large Stable Yard (partly paved) on three sides of which are the flowing stables etc. 20 Stall Stables with Loft and Corn Store over. Stable for 30 horses.

Also Stall Nag Stable with Harness Room, Coach House and 2 loose boxes.

A Smithy and Cooperage. Another 4 stall stables with man's room adjoining.

On the left hand side of the Entrance Yard opposite the Offices and Residences are the Loading Out Store and Four Beer Stores with vaulted Cellar below and a Garden with vaulted Beer Store under. The Site with Wells and Yard [much of this is unchanged today].

The greater part of this was owned freehold. Much of the remainder was held on a 99-year lease at an annual rent of £60.

The third deed of partnership was duly signed on 19 July 1887.

By then John Turner had already decided to retire, so the new agreement was between George Pargiter Fuller and Henry Smith, plus GP's son William Fleet-wood and Henry's nephew Frank Smith. But this combination was short-lived. Henry Smith died five months later, and John Turner in the following autumn. Smith's share went to his nephew Frank and his great-nephew Edward Trevelyan Turner, while Turner's went to his son by his second marriage, Robert Frederick Lewis. Though all this was arranged amicably enough, it is clear that the great problem of the succession was getting knottier with each year that passed.

THIS WAS SOON TO BE vividly demonstrated by an episode which started as a minor annoyance and was then whipped up into yet another constitutional storm.

It concerned the young Edward Trevelyan Turner – 'Trevy' to his family and to posterity. The son of J.E. Turner and the grandson of old John Turner, he grew up under a doting mother into what seems, if his behaviour is any guide, a rather selfish youth. No sooner had he become a very junior partner than he began requesting sums of money from the fund invested in his name. These grew from £100 in 1891 to £2,000 a year later.

In December 1893, the partners were flabbergasted to receive a demand from Trevy that he be allowed to retire from the business after only seven years. This was not just unprecedented: it was an affront to the spirit of the brewery. However, once they had recov-

and, by extension, pub landlords and brewers. In the early part of the 19th century, social reformers had seen spirits as the main problem and were happy for people to drink beer, as it was relatively weak and healthier than water, the latter being rarely pure. The rise of the teetotal movement changed this and all alcoholic drinks were branded dangerous; brewers for their part were grouped alongside distillers as a menace to society.

Luckily for the brewery, as Wheeler writes, 'there seemed to be little "temperance" in Chiswick but the prevalent conditions did not warrant such extremism. The area, as already noted, was "mixed" although perhaps still predominantly "middle-class"... however,

---

# DID YOU KNOW...

*The phrase 'ropey' has its origins in brewing, being applied to beer infected with bacteria that causes thin, gelatinous threads to appear.*

---

ered from the shock they realised that the loss would not be a great one. Trevy's resignation was accepted and made official with great alacrity.

Too late Trevy realised the rashness of his action. He wrote to the partners explaining that his mother had 'kicked up a bit' at his leaving the brewery and withdrawing his original request. His pleading was in vain. So were his various court actions against the partners: they were adamant in not wanting him back, and the law was on their side. By mid-1894 Trevy accepted defeat and made off with a good deal of umbrage – and his great-uncle's investment of £10,000.

There was one other aspect of late 19th-century life that could have had ramifications for the brewery – the issue of temperance. Victorian social reformers had long been shocked at what they deemed the abuse of drink among the working classes, especially in the big cities. Religious tracts, songs, etchings and friendship clubs were all drawn into the fight against drunkards

there could have been some "anxiety", for London was not too far away from Chiswick. Who was to know what the expansion of London might have brought to the area? A concern for the development of Chiswick has already been noted and perhaps prevention of any social situations conducive to excessive drinking was better than a cure which could have resulted in local antagonism towards the business of Messrs Fuller, Smith and Turner.'

Social movements would come and go with the frequency of autumn storms but the brewery would sail on through these disturbances, a solid, sturdy vessel on which the hopes of its owners and workers could depend.

# FULLER'S PUB PROFILE

# The Dove

**STAND OUTSIDE THE DOVE** and look towards the west and you will see Fuller's chimney reaching for the sky a mile away. Once comforted by the sight and reassured that all is well with the world, return to the dark-wooded bar of this venerable riverside pub and continue with your London Pride. The Dove has been here for centuries and during its reign has become a firm fixture of west London pub life (Fuller's have had it since the end of the 19th century). Anybody who has been anybody has sunk a jar within the walls of this paragon of solid Georgian architecture. The 18th-century poet and pub regular James Thomson reputedly wrote the words to 'Rule, Britannia!' here. William Morris also lived close by and probably brought his arts and crafts pals in for a noggin of good honest ale. Actors, poets, writers, conductors, scientists and even comedians have all made their way here. In the wrong hands the Dove could have ended up as a twee museum of London pub life. Thankfully, it didn't and remains a thoroughly civilised place offering the chance to soak up a sense of history, drink good beer and watch time and the river pass by.

THE DOVE, 19 UPPER MALL, LONDON W6 9TA

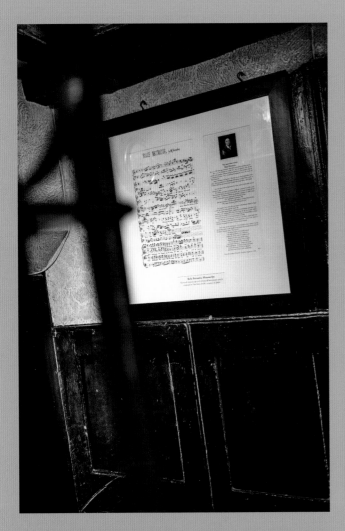

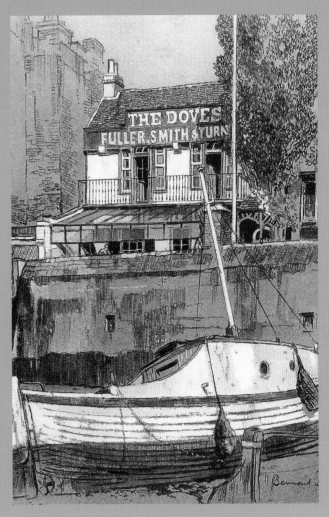

# TASTING NOTE
## WILD RIVER, 4.5%

THIS DOUBLE-HOPPED AMERICAN-STYLE PALE ALE was launched in 2012 with the hops all coming from the West Coast of the USA — Liberty, Willamette, Cascade and Chinook. Some might have said that this marked a departure for the brewery, but the brewing logs show that Fuller's was using American hops before the First World War, when they were jotted down under the name of Oregon. On the other hand, Wild River was definitely a new direction for Fuller's, in that it was inspired by the American craft beer revolution, but it also fitted easily into Fuller's portfolio. At the time, John Keeling said, 'There has been a huge growth in recent years within the craft beer movement, and we wanted to create our own interpretation of these full-flavoured hoppy beers. The selection of these four fantastic hops, and the infusion of their individual flavours through an innovative combination of hopping processes, has made this another exciting beer to work with.'

Light amber, veering towards dark gold, in colour; think of the glorious citrus aromatics that occur when a sharp knife scrapes the skin of a ripe orange and then a grapefruit and then a lime: the nose of this American-style pale ale is similar, zestful and cheerful, with a light undercurrent of honeyed graininess adding to the fun. More citrus emerges in the mouth, a soft medium sweetness, a clean mouth feel before a long dry and bittersweet finish.

# Spiced Rump of Texel White Lamb with Tarka Dhal, Pickled Cucumber and Yoghurt

Serves 10

## INGREDIENTS

| | |
|---|---|
| 5 | rumps Texel white lamb (or similar) |
| 150g | ras el hanout |

**For the tarka dhal:**

| | |
|---|---|
| 4 | shallots, sliced |
| 3 | garlic cloves, finely chopped |
| 100g | unsalted butter |
| 1 tbsp | ground coriander |
| 1 tbsp | mustard seeds |
| 2 tbsp | ground cumin |
| 1 tbsp | ground garam masala |
| 1 tsp | ground ginger |
| 1 tsp | ground turmeric |
| 1 tsp | chilli powder |
| 1kg | red lentils |
| 500g | tomato passata |
| 400g | drained chick peas |
| salt, to taste | |
| 40g | chopped fresh coriander |
| juice of 2 limes | |

**For the pickled cucumber:**

| | |
|---|---|
| 100ml | white wine vinegar |
| 100g | caster sugar |
| 5 | cumin seeds |

**To serve:**

| | |
|---|---|
| 400g | natural yoghurt |

## METHOD

To make the dahl, sweat the shallots and garlic gently in the butter until soft. Add the spices and cook for 1–2 minutes. Add the lentils and coat in the spiced mixture. Add the wine and allow to reduce. Add the tomato passata and chick peas and mix well. Pour in water to about 1cm above the lentils and bring to a simmer, then remove from the heat and cover – leave for about 10 minutes. Top up with water and bring back to a simmer, then remove from the heat and replace the lid – leave for 10 minutes. Repeat this process until the lentils are tender, then keep simmering the final time until the dhal is thick and not watery. Season to taste with salt and add the chopped coriander and lime juice.

For the pickled cucumber, place the pickling ingredients in a pan, bring to the boil and cool. Thinly slice the cucumber and marinate in the liquor for at least 20 minutes.

Meanwhile, preheat the oven to 180°C/fan oven 160°C/gas mark 4. Rub the lamb rumps in the ras el hanout, sear on all sides in a hot pan and roast in the preheated oven at 180°C for 15 minutes – the meat should be pink. Rest the lamb for about 10 minutes, keeping it warm.

To serve, slice the lamb (you should get 2 portions per rump) and place on a helping of dhal, garnished with pickled cucumber and topped with a spoonful of yoghurt.

# CHAPTER FOUR

# A New Century

**SLOWLY AND YET STATELY** the 19th century was reaching its inevitable demise, the end of an era perhaps, as there was so much change in the air. Some of it was technological, with developments such as the motorcar and the telephone destined to transform people's lives for good. There was also a sense of social change, as debates over votes for women made the headlines, while the Labour Party under Keir Hardie was starting to grow.

The British brewing industry was not impervious to this feeling of flux. By the end of the century the British were drinking less beer, with brewers blaming diversions such as music halls, football matches and cheap railway excursions as the culprits behind this trend. There was also a momentous change in the number of brewers making beer.

In 1870, there had been 133,840 licensed brewers in England and Wales, but by 1894 the number had declined to 9,664. Behind these figures, you could argue that the drop was not as catastrophic as the bald numbers suggested – the brewers going out of business worked mostly in small-scale or pub breweries, which were unable to compete with the mechanised plants, bulk prices and greater reliability of the big firms. In the late 1880s, there was also a trend for larger breweries to float themselves as public companies, which then gave them an ever-greater financial strength. However, the emergence of larger breweries brought forward a demand for more public houses, whose value doubled or in some cases trebled as availability declined. In London, nearly all pubs had become 'tied' houses by the end of the

century. So intense was the struggle that even more big brewers fell by the wayside. Others were forced to amalgamate (Mitchell's, for example, merging with Butler's in 1898).

At the same time, the public's taste in beer was changing. As mentioned before, porter was in terminal decline (though still being made) and the taste was for sparkling pale ales and India pale ales (both of which were brewed at Fuller's). Other beers found in Fuller's pubs, according to a price list from the end of the 19th century, would have included a Strong Old Ale, XK Bitter Pale Ale, AK Light Bitter Ale, X Amber Mild Ale and Double Stout. XK usually meant the ordinary bitter, while AK was a weaker version.

Choose the right pub selling Fuller's beers and the Victorian or Edwardian beer lover could have their very own beer festival! The same price list featured a run-down of the brewery's branch offices, including Brighton, Cardiff, Slough, Sandy and Southampton, which demonstrates the ambitions of Fuller's to reach out beyond their west London heartland.

Finally, this was also a time when the brewing industry, in tune with the Victorian love of exhibitions, embarked on its own celebration of a trade whose products many saw as the embodiment of the national character. The first Brewers' Exhibition was held in Islington, London, in 1879 and became an annual event, while 1888 saw a beer competition added, where eminent men in the industry passed judgment on their colleagues' beers. There is no evidence that Fuller's entered the competition in its

BREWERY WORKERS AT THE TURN OF THE CENTURY, POSE WITH THEIR TOOLS OF THE TRADE

opening years, but we can imagine that its brewery workers would have made the trip east to Islington to discover new technological advances and to taste the beers of breweries outside London.

IN THE MIDST OF THIS LIVELY PERIOD of brewing history, Fuller, Smith & Turner continued to thrive. Part of the reason would have been the sustained good quality of their beers, but as the modern age of communications dawned, the brewery assumed a more thoughtful approach to their marketing methods. For a start, the company took out a patent on the name 'Griffin', which had first been adopted by Douglas Thompson. Years had passed with little comment on the use, until a Mr T.P. Griffin objected to the brewery's unrestricted use of it (we don't know the reason for the objection – perhaps he was a Victorian version of compensation culture!). This action created a mountain of correspondence with the Board of Trade and the solicitors acting for both parties. However, by 1892 the matter was at last agreed and the trademark of the Griffin Brewery officially came into existence.

In a way, this official establishment of the Griffin trademark occurred at the right time. This was, after all, a period when breweries were sending more of their beer outside their traditional trading area and, as the aforementioned price list showed, Fuller, Smith & Turner were no different. To interest pub-goers who needed to be convinced of the goodness of a beer that they'd not heard of before, various means of promotion also had to be undertaken. These included branded calendars, show cards and posters, though come 1889 a more adventurous way of advertising emerged with the appearance of the Fuller's balloon.

The object was purchased by William Fuller, GP's second son, who had it emblazoned with the legend FULLER'S BEERS OF HONEST REPUTE in six-foot-high lettering. Given that this was on the cusp of the air age, William Fuller's purchase was exceptionally prescient and demonstrated an inventive mode of thinking. The balloon was flown for several years at Yarmouth Agricultural Show, at Windsor Races and at Kew or Hampton Court on bank holidays. At other times it floated imperiously over the brewery premises,

# ADVERTISING

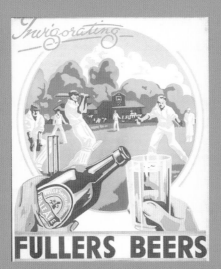

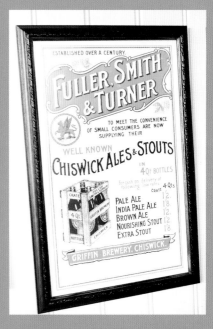

AS WILLIAM FULLER'S USE OF A BALLOON to advertise Fuller's beers demonstrated, the Victorian period saw breweries come of age in the way they publicised their beers. Sadly, there are no surviving photographs of the balloon at any of its sites, but old bottles embossed with the brewery's name, posters and labels remain, many on display in the Hock Cellar. Labels on beer bottles only became common towards the end of the 19th century, when many would be like mini works of art, especially as they were unencumbered by the need to include health warnings and suchlike. Advertising a product for a brewery like Fuller's changed through the 20th century: from bottle labels to bottle tops to posters and livery on the side of transport vehicles, all had their place in getting the name out.

leaving passers-by in no doubt about the forcefulness of the message.

**THERE WERE OTHER ROUTES** by which the brewery got its message out to the public. In November 1896, it achieved something of a publicity coup by being featured in a long-forgotten periodical called *Pictorial Review*. The magazine liked to boast of itself as a 'Compendium of Literature, Art, Fashion and Business Progress', and it was under the last of these headings that the article on Fuller's ran. Read over 100 years on, it is very much a product of its age, being over-wordy and self-important in its styling, but it is also a valuable historical document that gives a detailed description of work at the brewery.

The article opened with the arrival of the malt from the maltster's, which was then 'conveyed to the top of the building by means of a Jacob's Ladder, or endless band, of the shape only infinitely smaller than those we see used for dredging operations. The ladder travels through a closed shaft discharging the malt into a hopper or receiver on the top floor. The malt here passes through revolving brushes by which is it thoroughly cleaned. Then over a sieve fitted with magnets for attracting any particles of metal that might injure the steel rollers, through which it subsequently passes, and is ground.'

The writer also chose to focus on the device used for cooling the wort. 'It is passed over refrigerators and as this is a very ingenious apparatus... we will give a few words apropos. The refrigerators in question are a phalanx of metal tubes, presenting in appearance a Brobdingnagian washing board on the ribs of which the maid rubs the clothes on washing day... Through the inside of these tubes cold water is continually running, and over the outer surface the wort moves in a thin sheet extended over the whole mass of tubes.' To keep out impurities, these refrigerators were 'contained in an air-tight glass case, hermetically sealed'.

Despite the flowery prose and the overprecise descriptions of the brewing equipment and processes, the article managed to shine a light on several intriguing aspects of Fuller's. For instance, the writer commented on the gloomy store where old ale was kept in 'immense vats' to mature – some of it for over a year. Then there was the list of aristocratic households to which Fuller's supplied beer: this included the Prince of Wales (later Edward VII), the Duke of Edinburgh, Princess Victoria (the daughter of the old Queen), the Duke of Norfolk and the Duke of Marlborough. Finally, there was mention of the brewery's water, 'drawn from a well over 400 feet deep, the water from London chalk being gifted with unique brewing properties'.

The unnamed author of the *Pictorial Review*'s article painted a portrait of a gleaming, hyper-efficient, germ-free plant, producing faultless beer. This, unfortunately, was not quite correct. During the 1890s, the brewery received a growing number of complaints about the quality of Fuller's products, some of which were going off far too quickly in storage. George Pargiter was also worried by the amount of material being wasted in brewing and delivering. Far too great a percentage was being lost, he maintained in a letter: he made the point that when making jam at home, he allowed for only 3 per cent wastage during boiling.

**IT SEEMED CLEAR** that while the brewery's plant had grown more sophisticated, the brewer's techniques had lagged behind. Expert scientific advice was needed. This came in the shape of Dr Edward Ralph Moritz, an analytical chemist of German extraction. He specialised in the chemistry of brewing and in 1886 had been appointed as consultant to the Country Brewers' Society, a trade body that had been set up in 1822 and acted on behalf of regional brewers (in 1904 it would merge with the London Brewers' Society and the Burton Brewers' Society to form the Brewers' Society, which in turn became the current British Beer and Pub Association).

Shrewd, ambitious and formidably expert, Moritz was to have a considerable effect on the company's fortunes. His arrival brought with it a thoroughly 20th-century aura of white coats, test tubes and stainless steel – a piquant contrast to the cosy,

# DR EDWARD RALPH MORITZ 1860–1931

**DURING HIS LIFETIME,** London-born Edward Ralph Moritz was a towering presence on the English brewing scene, not only aiding Fuller's as they aimed to improve their beers, but helping other breweries too. He was also a prolific writer of books and papers and a canny businessman who was considerably wealthy at his death. As evidenced by his work with Fuller's, he was not shy in coming forward. According to Ray Anderson in *Brewers and Distillers by Profession*, which was published by the Institute of Brewing and Distilling in 2012, 'From February 1882 onwards hardly a month passed without an article or letter from him appearing in the trade press on some aspect of brewing... an advertisement of the time illustrates that he was also happy for his judgment to be used by brewers to illustrate the "soundness" of their beers. A testimonial supplied to Messrs Hanley Brothers, City Brewery, Oxford, waxes lyrical on how the firm's Bitter Ale is: "... prepared from *pure malt* and *hops* alone, and that neither sugars nor other malt substitutes, nor bitter drugs, or so called hop substitutes have been employed in its manufacture. It is pure unadulterated Beer, thoroughly sound and palatable, wholesome and nutritious."'

# TRANSPORT

**YOU CAN IMAGINE IT:** a cold winter's day sometime in the early 1900s. The yard at the Griffin Brewery, the bang of wooden barrels being loaded on to a dray, the curses and the calls of the men at work and the patience of the horses as they waited to head off on their daily round. In the murk of the early morning, the flash of orange sparks as their steel-shod hoofs struck the stone beneath them as they headed out. Until the 1930s, Fuller's still maintained a sense of Chiswick's semi-rural past with its herd of dray-horses, which if we look at a Fuller's photograph from later on in the 1930s would have been the classic shire horse of English legend. And then came the steam wagons first of all, followed by the petrol-fuelled lorries and the end of an era – though one can still see beautiful shire horses pulling drays in Fuller's livery at various shows. The past doesn't always have to shuffle away and vanish.

wood-panelled Victorian world of the partners. He was also a well-regarded author on brewing matters.

The first thing the company asked Dr Moritz to do was to investigate the matter of the wastage. His report back was prompt and thorough. The brewing plant, he said, was not in a satisfactory state and he offered to make a more detailed investigation, recommend the necessary alterations and personally supervise the implementation of these recommendations. His fee for this would be £525. Furthermore, he suggested that afterwards he should be retained as an independent consultant. There was obviously nothing diffident about Dr Moritz.

Moritz's style impressed the partners and his estimates that the necessary improvements to the brewery would cost £6,500 were accepted without demur – at least publicly. In private, the partners were concerned about the reaction of the incumbent head brewer, John Storey. Would he take offence at the open criticism of his work and at the interference of an outsider? He clearly didn't and in June 1900 an agreement was signed, retaining the services of Moritz for a period of 20 years.

The energetic doctor wasted no time in bringing modern science to bear on the deteriorating quality of the 'Griffin Brew'. He discovered that one of the main problems was the poor standard of the malt, which was causing brews to 'go off'. His solution was simple, if daunting: the firm must manufacture its own malt, building a brand-new maltings for the purpose. When the partners had regained their breath, they discussed the matter and eventually gave their consent to this bold scheme. They approached the Duke of Devonshire's agent and enquired about the price of a stretch of land upriver at Duke's Meadows. It was £1,500. By November 1900, the land had been purchased and proposals for the maltings buildings had been drawn up, with various builders invited to tender for the contract.

Another shock awaited the partners when the tenders arrived. The builders' estimates varied between £33,000 and £39,000, exclusive of machinery, which would take the total cost up to well over £40,000. George Pargiter was firm in not countenancing such expenditure and he instructed Dr Moritz to meet the architect and try to reduce the costs. At the next partners' meeting, Moritz presented a revised estimate of £23,550. But GP was still not satisfied. Finally, in April 1902, a building contract was signed for £18,430: the work to be completed within 42 weeks.

This was the beginning of a fresh nightmare for the partners. As building work began and demands for expenses rose, they must have feared that Moritz's dynamism had driven them along too fast. Not only were they saddled with a complex new enterprise that was soaking up their working capital and forcing them to raise a new mortgage, but there were other financial worries too. They had become liable for the debts of their hotel at Drayton Court (making yet another mortgage necessary) and the beginnings of a national recession had caused a slump in beer sales, which wouldn't pick up until 1909.

GP was something of an amateur statistician and a compulsive scribbler of notes. Now, during this most

**A YOUTHFUL AND RELAXED JOHN FULLER**

STAFF OUTING FOR FEMALE BREWERY WORKERS IN 1919 WITH PLENTY OF FLAGS CELEBRATING THE END OF THE FIRST WORLD WAR
(*BELOW*) THE BOTTLING HALL AND RACKING ROOM IN THE 1930S

active and anxious time of the brewery's life, we can imagine him sitting in his study at Neston Park, feverishly juggling with percentages and calculations, which were aimed at making economies in the various brewery departments. His main concern in life had been to launch his five sons on suitable careers and for this to happen they needed stable incomes from the brewery.

John, the eldest, was already a successful politician, and was to become Liberal MP for Westbury between 1900 and 1911 before being appointed governor of the Australian state of Victoria. William and Henry had been working as managers at the Griffin Brewery since the 1890s, although William apparently was much more interested in hunting and cricket than brewing. He kept a pack of beagles next to the bottling store and it was the delight of employees to lure the hounds into the store and get them drunk. Robert had bought a rubber company in Wiltshire (later to become Avon Rubber), while Edward, the youngest, had been established on the plantation of the Abbotsleigh Tea Company in what was then called Ceylon.

The brothers depended, to differing extents, upon the good health of the brewery. They each had ideas for helping the business out of its present crisis and communicated them to one another in a good-natured way. After one encouraging letter from his eldest brother, Henry wrote back, 'any appreciation of one's endeavour to put the business on a sound footing is most pleasant to a sensitive ass like me'. However, when the suggestion was made that the business should be turned into a limited company, both John and his father quickly squashed it.

### MEANWHILE, OVER IN THE LABORATORY,

Dr Moritz was dreaming up his own schemes for reviving profitability – though these typically involved

the spending as well as the making of money. One was a duplication of existing brewing plant, which he insisted to the partners would save hops to the value of £1,000 a year. Another was a new wonder brew called Protene Stout, which he had just invented. The partners, as always mesmerised by the doctor's enthusiasm, not only bought the formula for the beer but paid out extra money so that he could set up some experimental equipment for the brew. However, Protene Stout was not to change the fortunes of Fuller's, for after some initial excitement it vanished from the agenda.

George Pargiter was now in his seventies, but his hold on the reins was as firm as ever. When the expiration of the latest deed of partnership loomed in 1906, there was much heated talk about amalgamating with another brewery. GP was deeply upset. 'This sweeping departure', he wrote, 'from a policy carried out now for more than two generations, with what must be allowed to be extraordinary success and amity, positively alarmed me. I therefore felt bound to put in a veto... I am sure that you will feel when the time comes for providing occupation, remunerative as well as honourable, for the rising generation of the Fuller family how valuable a family concern is to the happy fathers and mothers.'

These words have a particular resonance today, since Fuller's has survived – against all the commercial odds – as a family concern.

However, GP's defiance must have seemed unrealistic at the time given the financial situation. In 1906, the firm's debts stood at a staggering £220,000, with annual interest of 4.5 per cent. Then another expense was about to be incurred. The original well had never provided enough water for the brewery and had had to be supplemented from the mains. Over the next six years engineers drilled away in an attempt to find a satisfactory new borehole. By 1912 they had reached a depth of 1,300 feet, but no water was found and the scheme was abandoned (rumour has it that sometime later on in the 20th century, the well became contaminated by yeast from a nearby bakery).

Apparently undeterred by this constant leaching of cash, the partners extended their interests. In 1909, they purchased William Gomm & Son's Beehive Brewery in Brentford, which was located at the meeting of the backwaters of the Thames and the Grand Junction Canal. Fuller's did not need the brewery itself, which was sold off in lots, but their real gain was a total of 34 pubs, mostly free- or copyhold, which greatly increased the available outlets for Fuller's beers.

This was not Fuller's first attempt at buying breweries. Back in 1897 and 1898 three breweries were

At this point Dr Moritz returns to the story with yet another bright idea, his latest project being something he called 'the secret process'. According to the minutes of a partners' meeting, he asked leave for 'H.F. Fuller, Frank Smith and R.F.L. Turner to interest themselves in a syndicate for the manufacture of Extract of Malt'. Leave was granted and for some months a furtive air surrounded the subject. Dr Moritz was busy applying for a patent and searching for a suitable name. This was more difficult than he imagined and he began to lose patience. To the partners he wrote, 'You could call it "the Starch Dissolving Products Company" but that would give too much away. Call it what you like, I don't really care!' After some false starts, they settled on the professional title of Solutal.

The new company began producing Solutal on brewery premises during 1911, using, one assumes, malt as the basic ingredient. Such was the need for

---

# DID YOU KNOW...

**The first trademark to be registered in Britain was on 1 January 1876, and it was the red triangle that Bass Brewery used on the labels of their India Pale Ale.**

---

bought: the Dagnall Brewery in Dagnall, Berkshire, W.H. Complin in Southampton, and the more local Dobell & Courtauld, which like the Beehive was based in Brentford. Dagnall and Complin came with a pub estate, though in subsequent years the partners seemed to have not made much of the purchase. Dagnall's 24 pubs were let to Locke & Smith of Berkhamsted in 1905 and eventually sold off in 1913; meanwhile, Complin's pubs were eventually bought by Courage after the First World War. The third brewery, Dobell & Courtauld, was only bought after it had been destroyed by fire.

In the present day, Richard Fuller professes himself mystified by the two non-local purchases. 'Why did we decide to buy breweries in Dagnall and Southampton', he asks, 'and then they disappeared without trace? What was the business model?'

secrecy that the exact nature of the product was not recorded anywhere, but it seems that a kind of starch was manufactured, which was sold on to laundries in the area, which seems rather strange given that its original intended use was to help with brewing. Solutal had some initial success, but by 1915 complaints were beginning to pour in. One laundry in particular pointed out that it was discolouring their linen. A shortage of funds, made worse by the death of the wealthy Frank Smith in 1912, meant that no more research could be done. Solutal slowly dropped out of sight and became a minor and mysterious footnote in the history of the brewery.

**HOWEVER, WHILE MORITZ INVESTIGATED** the properties of Solutal, there was a more pressing problem in the outside world, when an Austrian archduke was assassinated in the Bosnian city of Sarajevo,

# INGREDIENTS FOR BREWING
# BARLEY

A GLASS OF BEER BEGINS ITS LIFE in a field of golden barley swaying in a gentle breeze before harvest intrudes and brutally ends the life of John Barleycorn. The farmer's work done, the grains are whisked away to a maltings and the first step of the transformative journey of brewing begins. The skill of the maltsters is to start germination in the grains, producing enzymes that break down the starch within each kernel into soluble malt sugars. However, before full self-regeneration can be achieved, the process is stopped and the grain is kilned, producing malted barley; some barley grains are roasted for longer to darken their colour and deepen the flavour, while crystal malt is produced by a process similar to toffee-making. Now it's off to the brewery. Here, crushed and ground malt (the grist) is steeped in hot water in the mash tun and the run-off is called wort, a creamy Ovaltine-coloured liquid full of those oh-so-pliant malt sugars that will eventually be devoured by yeast during fermentation, with alcohol and $CO_2$ being produced. The next step: the drinker's glass.

# BREWING TASKMASTERS

BREWING HAS ALWAYS BEEN A PHYSICAL OCCUPATION, though the advent of computer-controlled systems that regulate water flow, control the temperature of the mash and even empty the mash tun has changed things somewhat. In the years before the First World War brewing was a hard, muscular job: cleaning the fermenting vessels would have been a two-man role – one inside and one outside to keep an eye on his mate, just to make sure he wouldn't be overcome by any lingering fumes of carbon dioxide. In the racking area, 18-gallon wooden casks would have had beer pumped into them by workers holding oversized hoses. After returning casks had been cleaned, there would have been a man whose job it was to sniff the empty ones to make sure that no infections or impurities remained inside. The head brewer usually began the first mash early in the morning and there was a long tradition in the industry of a 'brewer's breakfast' – a raw egg engulfed in a glass of sweet wort. In an age when beer was supplied in wooden casks, Fuller's and other similar-sized breweries had their own cooperage, where casks were mended and made. Draymen looked after horses as well as leading them on deliveries in all weathers; carpenters, electricians, bottlers and even part-time firemen all reported for duty at a brewery over a century ago.

a place that few if any at the brewery had ever heard of. The Great War of 1914–18 began and the brewery faced a fresh set of problems. For a start, a growing number of employees (and partners) enlisted in the armed forces, leaving an acute shortage of labour. This forced the company to take the revolutionary step of employing women. By the end of the war, there were 27 female labourers at work in the bottling and mineral plants.

In the outside world, beer sales fell drastically and government interference in the licensed trade verged on the authoritarian. Prime Minister Lloyd George was anti-alcohol and he declared that 'drink is causing more damage in the war than all the German submarines put together'; he also persuaded King George V to go dry for the duration. The Defence of the Realm Act, which limited pub opening hours, was brought into force, while it was deemed illegal to 'treat' servicemen to a beer. As for the national drink, this became weaker, with an original gravity of 1030° being common for most beers (before the First World War original gravities had ranged from 1055° for porter to 1048° for mild). In Chiswick, matters had grown so serious by 1917 that Fuller's signed an agreement to share resources with three nearby rivals – the Isleworth Brewery, the Lamb Brewery (Sich & Co) and the Victoria Brewery in Windsor.

This arrangement continued until the Armistice in November 1918, when the four went their separate ways. But Sich & Co never recovered their pre-war prosperity. In 1921, after protracted negotiations, they sold their premises and business to Watney, Combe & Reid, who kept the valuable portfolio of pubs and sold the land and buildings on to Fuller, Smith & Turner for £23,400. Without the tied houses, the purchase was of limited value, although it gave room to expand the brewery slightly. Like a shadow of the past, the Sich name can still be seen faintly on the wooden tower to the west of the present site. Meanwhile, with the war over, Fuller's could progress into the peace, though what the future held none of the board could know.

A RARE INSTANCE OF ISLEWORTH BREWERY-EMBOSSED WINDOWS ONCE FOUND IN A FORMER PUB OF THEIRS

# The Drayton Court Hotel

**THE DRAYTON CAN BE FOUND** amid the leafy streets of Victorian and Edwardian villas, a late 19th-century hotel fantasy of Gothic turrets and towers. Fuller's opened it in 1894, bringing an architectural lushness into a calm and considered world that would vanish with the Great War (it's ironic that one of the great revolutionaries of the 20th century, Ho Chi Minh, once did a stint in the kitchens here in 1914; some whisper about a Masonic temple hidden away below as well). Even though locals probably propped up the hotel bar, it was only in the 1940s that it gained a licence to act as a pub as well, a double act that it performs so adeptly now, especially after its 2011 renovation. Inside, the large main bar has snapshots of the building from the early part of the 1900s, while there's also a less bustling room to the left of the entrance. However, when the sun shines it's to the back garden that people go, a glass of Oliver's Island in hand; and out here, lost among the grass lawn, tables and benches, the flower beds and kids' playing area, it's possible to get away from the hustle and bustle of London without going anywhere near the M4. It was once rumoured to be the biggest pub garden in the country – but we really aren't sure that this fact still holds true today!

THE DRAYTON COURT HOTEL, 2 THE AVENUE, LONDON W13 8PH

# TASTING NOTE

# PAST MASTERS 1910 DOUBLE STOUT, 7.4%

THE PAST MASTERS SERIES stems from John Keeling's curiosity about the beers that have been produced by Fuller's since the three families joined forces in 1845. He has a wealth of information to go on, as there are stacks of meticulously kept brewing logs that go back to the 19th century, treasure-troves of rare beers that were popular before the First World War. Keeling not only aims to replicate the brewing processes of the past but tries as accurately as possible to use similar raw materials, though given the developments in barley and hops over the century this is much harder.

Since starting the series he has produced a Double Stout from 1893, an XX Strong Ale from 1891, an Old Burton Extra from 1931, a Strong X that according to the log books was first brewed on 4 August 1914 (the day Britain declared war on Germany) and, to demonstrate that not all the Past Masters beers lie in the distant past, a 1966 Strong Ale. This last one was originally brewed to celebrate England winning the World Cup. When it was brewed, Keeling was assisted by a member of the brewing team involved in the first brew, who at the time of the brew in 2013 was still very much active at the brewery. The 1910 Double Stout was 2015's addition to the range, a rich and dark strong stout brewed at the end of the Edwardian age, the style of beer which, before the First World War, doctors had no hesitation in prescribing to 'invalids' (they were also happy to provide signed testimonials to the efficacy of this kind of beer).

As dark as the darkest night in the glass, though with a crimson tint to its edges, the first thing to celebrate is the waft of chocolate and coffee notes coming off the nose, powerful and potent, drawing in the drinker. There are more helpings of chocolate and coffee on the palate, alongside ripe autumn berries and a powerful bitterness in the finish. This beer and others in the series are remarkable parts of Fuller's brewing history and heritage.

## PERFECT WITH FULLER'S
## PAST MASTERS 1910 DOUBLE STOUT

# London Porter Smoked Salmon with Golden Pride Sourdough, Lemon and Raspberries

Serves 1

### INGREDIENTS

| | |
|---|---|
| 1 | lemon |
| 150g | sugar |
| 100g | Golden Pride Sourdough (or plain sourdough) |
| 100g | London Porter Smoked Salmon, D Cut Side (or similar) |
| 12g | pickled raspberries (see Method) |
| | baby basil cress, to garnish |

For the fruit pickle:

| | |
|---|---|
| 500ml | Cornish Orchards Vintage Cider |
| 200ml | cider vinegar |
| 600g | caster sugar |
| 5g | whole garlic clove |
| 5 | coriander seeds |
| ½ tsp | Maldon sea salt |
| 6 | white peppercorns |
| 4 | sprigs oregano |
| 3 | sprigs thyme |
| 2 | vanilla pods |

### METHOD

Put all the pickling ingredients into a heavy-based saucepan and bring to the boil, then turn down the heat and simmer for 5 minutes. Remove from the stove and allow to cool. Once the liquor has cooled, use it to pickle soft fruits such as raspberries (as we've used here), gooseberries, blueberries etc. Place the berries of your choice in Kilner jars, pour over the pickling liquor, then seal the jars and keep refrigerated while you prepare the rest of the dish.

Next, segment the lemon. First, use a sharp peeler to peel the lemon – retain the skin. Then use a sharp knife to cut off the top and bottom so that the lemon sits upright on a chopping board. Carefully 'peel' down the lemon one strip at a time, revealing the meaty part and leaving no skin or pith behind, repeating all the way round. Carefully cut into either side of each segment, so that it comes away, continuing until you have segmented the whole lemon.

To make the candied lemon, place the peeled skin on a chopping board and slice very thinly. Put the slices in a pan of cold water and bring to the boil. Once boiled, strain the lemon and put back into a pan of fresh water, then repeat this process once more. Once the lemon has been blanched, place in a pan with the sugar and 100ml water and bring to a simmer over medium heat. Simmer for 1 minute, then remove from the heat and allow to cool.

Slice the sourdough into a nice even medium slice and toast under the grill or in a toaster. Top with 3 slices of smoked salmon folded over to give some height, and serve garnished with a few pickled raspberries, some baby basil cress, lemon peel and lemon segments.

# CHAPTER FIVE

# The Winds Of Change

**WITH THE END OF THE WAR** to end all wars, as the optimists called the First World War, the landscape of British brewing had changed as irrevocably as that of wartorn northern France. Duty rates had soared, while the strength of British beer had plummeted. There was one bright ray of sunshine, though: the vocal temperance lobby had failed to persuade the government to follow the USA's example of prohibition.

The moderate strength of British beer hadn't escaped the notice of a *Brewers Journal* correspondent in 1921 when commenting on an award-winning beer at that year's Brewers' Exhibition: 'In offering our congratulations to Messrs. Aitken on their success, we think it reflects considerable credit on the brewers' skill that a beer of such low gravity should be adjudged worthy of the highest award.' Other commentators in the brewing press noted the growing popularity of light-coloured bottled beers that were chilled, filtered and carbonated (this was in contrast to what were called naturally conditioned beers, which could be seen to be the equivalent of today's bottle-conditioned beers).

The trend for clean and light flavours was mirrored in the way British pubs were being reorganised, as brewers felt the need to 'improve' their estates in order to attract more women (with their boyfriends or husbands) and younger drinkers. There still remained a common perception among non-regular pub-goers that the public house was dingy and insalubrious, and the new type of pub design was in response to this. It was nicknamed 'Brewers' Tudor': pubs often had a mock baronial hall makeover, while inside there was a move away from snugs and hidden corners and towards bringing more light and air into the interior.

Fuller's would not have been immune to these post-war changes. One can imagine, for instance, that the great stately strong brews of the late Victorian and Edwardian era became too impractical to make, as the high rates of duty would have rendered them off-puttingly expensive in pubs. This meant the suspension of brewing beers such as Double Stout or the robust XX Strong Ale, both of which have recently been resurrected under the banner of Past Masters.

Along with these changes in the kind of beers brewed and the appearance of the pub, brewery transport underwent a similar progression, though this was more about technological advances rather than governmental interference. One morning in the early 1920s, a Foden steam wagon puffed its way into the brewery yard and probably alarmed the drayhorses (there had been an earlier trial of steam wagons at the turn of the century with a locally built Thornycroft vehicle, but nothing had come of this). The vehicle remained on hire for eight months from the Western Motor Transport Company, costing £5 a day with an addition of ten shillings an hour for any overtime use after 5pm. Even though the cost must have seemed fairly daunting, an order was sent to Foden's London agents for 'two 5 ton steam wagons costing £1,160 each with standard body – delivery in three months' time'. Clearly, this noisy newcomer had proved its worth and the era of drayhorse-delivered beers was drawing to its natural end, though it wasn't until 1936 that steam lorries finally assumed full responsibility for brewery deliveries.

THE END OF THE DRAYHORSE ERA IS NIGH WITH THE APPEARANCE OF A FODEN STEAM WAGON

There was also change among the partners. In 1922 Dillwyn Fuller, son of Henry Fleetwood, resigned his partnership in the company and went off to join Dr Moritz and his nephew in their consultancy. Outside observers might have felt some surprise at this decision, but those on the inside would not have. Apparently, Dillwyn had not enjoyed his life at the brewery, while relations with his father were often strained. So it can be concluded that his departure was a relief to all. Dr Moritz himself retired a few years later.

In 1924, Major Robert Frederick Lewis Turner, youngest son of John Turner, died at his Wimbledon home. He had been called in as a very young man to help run the brewery and been a partner for over three decades; one of his achievements had been overseeing the start-up of the estate department, which built and maintained the various properties. His funeral was held at St Nicholas, Chiswick, and was attended by family members, brewery staff

and several tenants. The 'Last Post' and 'Reveille' were sounded over the grave by trumpeters of the Honourable Artillery Company.

The following year saw an intriguing departure from the unwritten law of the Fuller succession, when two new partners were admitted. One was Edward Hamilton Fleetwood Fuller, George Pargiter's grandson (and son of Edward, the tea planter); he went on to become the first company secretary and second chairman. The other was Philip Stirling Eliot, prospective husband of Henry's daughter Joyce. Here was a conundrum. Henry obviously had his daughter's best interests at heart, but the admission of someone from outside the immediate family was not strictly permitted under the articles of partnership.

Once again, agitated letters flew backwards and forwards between the partners and counsel's opinion was called for. Legal documents were drafted and redrafted. Everyone insisted upon one immutable

MAJOR ROBERT FREDERICK LEWIS TURNER, A PARTNER FOR OVER 30 YEARS AND CREATOR OF THE BREWERY'S ESTATE DEPARTMENT

HENRY FLEETWOOD FULLER, THE FIRST CHAIRMAN OF FULLER, SMITH & TURNER WHEN IT BECAME A PRIVATE LIMITED COMPANY IN 1929

clause: that the share should remain with Joyce in the event of her fiancé's death. This would surely prevent any 'outsiders' having a possible claim on the brewery. Henry Fuller wrote, 'Should there be no children to the marriage, I do not wish either party to have the power to appoint the share in business away from the Fuller family.' Even now the Thompson brothers were casting their grim shadow. Happily, Eliot proved to be a tower of quiet, unassuming strength and his extensive legal knowledge became invaluable.

However, the most monumental change of all was reported on 12 April 1927 in a simple sentence from the minutes: 'The Partners have to report, with sincere regret, the death of Mr G.P. Fuller.' George Pargiter had been born during the reign of William IV and was 12 years old when the partnership of Fuller, Smith & Turner was formed. For over half a century he had been the 'father' of the partners, wielding enormous influence. Though Liberal in politics, he had believed unbendingly in the traditional values of the partnership

and set his face against the invasive world of financial share dealing. He had been a link with the old way of brewing and the brave new world of the 19th century, and his passing would have been mourned by all in the brewery, as well as in the wider brewing community.

WITH THE PASSING OF GP, the way at last lay open for Fuller, Smith & Turner to be registered as a private limited company. This duly occurred on 22 August 1929. It involved procedures of transfer which are standard for such a process, but read over 80 years on still manage to have a vague whisper of farce: one memorandum read, 'an agreement for sale was entered into between Fuller, Smith & Turner and Fuller, Smith & Turner Ltd'. However, there was nothing risible about the 'consideration to be paid thereon', which was £1 million. The partners of the old firm, including William, Henry and Edward (Tony) Fuller, Alan Russell Smith, head brewer R.J.B. Storey and Philip Eliot, became the directors of the new, with their first meeting held on 18 September. Henry Fuller was made chairman.

# COOPERS' INITIATION CEREMONY

FULLER'S COOPERS HAD THEIR INITIATION CEREMONIES, which were probably the same as those at cooper-ages up and down the country. Prior to an apprentice qualifying as a cooper, there was one last hurdle to overcome: he would be put in a barrel and all manner of liquids and wood shavings would be poured over him, before the barrel was tipped on its side and rolled about with the young man inside. Messy it may have been, but it was a threshold crossed, a ceremony that made the newcomer feel part of the team. Naturally, a few beers would have been drunk in celebration afterwards. Fuller's cooperage closed several decades ago as metal casks replaced their wooden counterparts, but with this photograph from 1956 we can reimagine the anarchic but good-natured sense of the occasion – the man in the barrel is one Tom Wood, while the chap on the left holding the bag of shavings from on-high is a Dennis Sullivan. Note the (unnamed) cooper on the left with the hammer – presumably his job was to make a racket on the barrel as it was rolled about.

The first share authorised 300,000 preference shares and 6,000 ordinary shares. The brewery had moved into a new and far more profitable era.

Meanwhile, another development outside the company was being planned, which would have a massive, though less direct, influence on its future. This was the new Great West Road, which was intended to open up a fast route to the west and bring relief to the old High Road in Chiswick. It was an idea that had been floating around since the horse-and-carriage days of the 19th century and was a natural consequence of London's growth.

On the face of it, the partners might have felt that the brewery would lose out, as the new road would carve straight through the community, cutting off the Griffin premises and the old Chiswick riverfront from the rest of Chiswick. There might be a sense of dislocation from their heartland and with it a loss of identity. Happily,

brought Fuller, Smith & Turner more and more into the modern world of brewing.

**AT THE START OF 1930** a further sign of forward thinking came when the directors signed a new 14-year contract with Moritz and Partners. The Moritz in question was not the doctor, but his nephew Francis; one of his partners was, of course, Dillwyn Fuller. Dr Moritz had long been retired and a few months later he died. There is no doubt that his expert advice and enthusiasm had transformed the quality of Fuller's beer since the late 1890s. During this time (according to the 'appreciation' of Moritz in the minute book), the firm's profits had risen from £18,000 to £60,000. A glowing obituary in the *Journal of the Institute of Brewing* spoke of his 'inspiring incentive to individualism'.

One of Moritz's most successful legacies was Corney Road's maltings. It had undergone an expensive birth,

# DID YOU KNOW...

*A fear of an empty beer glass is called cenosillicaphobia.*

instead of marooning Fuller's, it was to prove, in years to come, a blessing – if nothing else there would be the free publicity provided by the sight of the brewery, its name bright and bold, as traffic came into London, a view that still greets travellers today.

However, there was some immediate inconvenience when Middlesex county council began issuing compulsory purchase orders to clear the way for digging. In 1928, the brewery had to sell off a strip of land fronting Mawson Lane (part of the Lamb Brewery's garden). A year later, the estate yard, van yard, carpenter's shop and cottages to the north of Mawson Lane had gone. Doubtless, there would have been disruption, but it could be argued that once the road was finished brewery transport could move east and west with greater ease. At the end of the decade, the coming of the Great West Road (which was built in stages), along with the establishment of the private limited company,

while some at the brewery had been doubtful of its necessity, but it had grown into a thriving adjunct to the business, with increasing profits year by year. By the early 1930s, it was producing over 17,000 quarters of malt annually (four quarters made one imperial hundredweight). In 1932, the Maltings became a private limited company, separate from the brewery, and the parent company leased the site to Fuller's Maltings Limited for an annual rent of £500.

However, amid these positive developments and successes there was stormy economic weather ahead. In 1929 the Wall Street Crash shook the western world and the brewing industry did not escape the problems caused by the resulting Great Depression. Every unemployed worker meant one less customer able to afford a pint in the pub; fewer customers in pubs meant less beer being sold and brewed. The move from cask beer to bottled beer also continued,

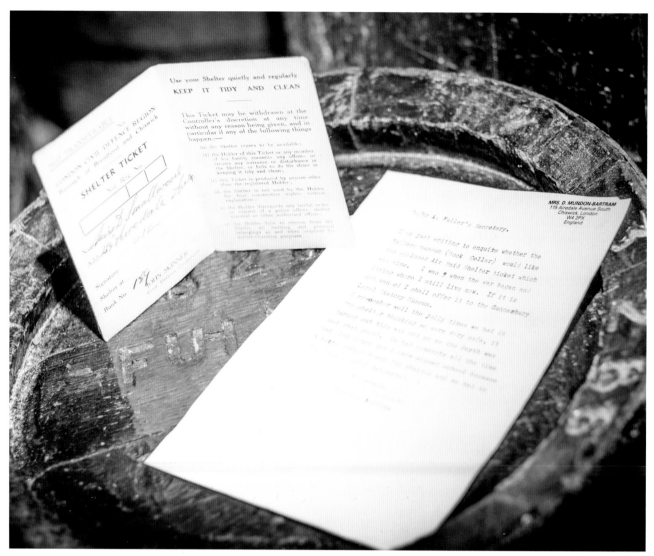

A YOUNG DOROTHY BARTRAM'S SHELTER TICKET FOR THE HOCK CELLAR

as exemplified by a report on the Brewers' Exhibition in 1930 by a *Brewing Trade Review* correspondent: 'The constant increase in the sales of bottled beer and decrease in cask beer were both demonstrable in the great preponderance of bottling plant on display, both old and new.'

In 1931, the Labour government crumbled, unable to control the sliding economy. Among its less popular achievements was a 40 per cent rise in beer duty, which put an extra penny on a pint, a measure that helped the national consumption of beer to fall by 20 per cent from what it was in the 1920s. Such was the mood of the time that some brewers were asking themselves the question: could beer survive?

With this environment, trade at the Griffin Brewery was badly hit in the downturn. The dividend on ordinary

shares for the nine months to 31 December 1932 fell to 5 per cent and the directors were forced to take drastic measures. Wages were reduced by 10 per cent and the brewery was shut on Saturdays. It was not until the same period in 1934 that things returned to normal and the ordinary shares dividend inched its way back to 11 per cent.

At the same time, the brewing community launched a fightback, with the Brewers' Society, of which Fuller's was a member, commissioning an advertising campaign of posters on which the slogan 'Beer is Best' shone out like a beacon of conviviality. There were various illustrations, from simple, thirst-creating ones showing a glass of sparkling, refreshing-looking beer to the frankly surreal – a horse made from a beer barrel, being ridden by Mr XXX, a beer glass with a human face. This campaign continued into the 1950s.

HOWEVER, THOSE CASTING THEIR EYES over the Channel could see that there were bigger problems on the horizon and Fuller, Smith & Turner Limited was barely ten years old when Britain declared war on Germany in September 1939. Temperance campaigners once more argued for controls on beer and pubs similar to those in the First World War, but calmer heads were in control this time – the government realised the morale-lifting benefits of a pint (albeit much weaker and often in short supply) down the pub.

At Fuller's, various emergency measures were quickly taken. The Hock Cellar was transformed into an air-raid shelter for up to 800 people: its roof was reinforced and bunks were fitted. Special shelter tickets were issued and a young Dorothy Bartram (née Smallwood) was one of those taking refuge there. Years later, she wrote to the brewery and donated her shelter ticket to the display of brewery artefacts in the Hock Cellar. In her accompanying letter she wrote, 'I remember well the jolly times we had in the shelter thinking we were very safe. It turned out this was not so as the depth was not that great. We had concerts all the time and sang songs and I once missed school because 5 bombs dropped around the shelter and we had to stay inside until detonated.'

On the night of 10 October 1940, German bombs hit the maltings and the building was gutted by fire, destroying most of the plant and stock. Elsewhere, an off-licence was demolished, while over 30 pubs suffered damage. There was no let-up in the bombing and more properties were hit. In December, another firebomb attack damaged the brewery premises and destroyed further public houses.

Several of the brewery's employees worked as firewatchers during the Blitz. One night a firebomb landed close to the Mawson Arms. It was soon dowsed with sand and little damage was done. The firewatchers were officially commended for the swiftness of their response. Nobody thought to point out that they had all been inside the Mawson Arms at the time.

ONE OF THE BREWERS' SOCIETY'S MORE SURREAL 'BEER IS BEST' POSTERS

Meanwhile, many staff volunteered for the forces. Special leave of absence was granted for four of the directors (Philip Eliot, Edward and Christopher Fuller and Lewis Turner), who joined up. The quartet served throughout the war years and returned safely to the company. Scores of employees also joined up: by 1945 there were 78 on active service.

Bombs, the blackout and a shortage of labour and materials – all these factors forced the directors into cutting back production. In May 1941, the supply of bottled beer to on-licence houses and clubs was reduced by a third (cask beer was also rationed later on). By the autumn of 1942, the workforce was so shorn that office hours were increased to 46 a week and brewery ones to 52.

One small item in the minute book for 1943 stands out simply because it is so unusual. It is headed 'theft of beer T.H. Fraser' and reported that said Fraser, one of the draymen, had been found guilty at Acton police

AFTER STEAM CAME FODEN DIESEL LORRIES, ONE OF WHICH IS SEEN HERE LOADED WITH BARRELS

CARD CELEBRATING A STAFF CRUISE UP THE THAMES FOR THE
QUEEN'S CORONATION IN 1953

court of stealing beer from the brewery. Presumably he never worked for Fuller's again.

From June 1944 a new danger appeared in the skies: flying bombs. First it was the V-1, or doodlebug. Then V-2 rockets started to fall all over London, with the very first landing in Staveley Road, just around the corner from the brewery. Before hostilities ceased, the brewery itself was hit twice more, though with little serious effect. By the end of the war, over 70 Fuller's pubs and off-licences had suffered bomb damage. Despite this the company continued to prosper – the accounts for 1944 showed a profit of over £158,000.

Naturally, the VE and VJ Day celebrations in 1945 gave the brewery a fine opportunity to further boost sales. When VE Day occurred, on 8 May, a special notice to the staff was pinned up, asking for volunteers: 'Owing to the particular position of the Brewing Industry in relation to the public on such an occasion like this, the Directors hope that in order to meet the demands of the situation, a skeleton staff will be willing to work on VE Day and the following day.'

Even though the fighting had stopped, it heralded a long period of adjustment and clearing up. Bomb-damaged properties were renovated or rebuilt, though there was little that could be done with the burnt-out maltings. Meanwhile, the serving directors and employees returned from active duty to their brewery positions. By 1947, all but 17 were back in harness. Looking back on the post-war reintegration of former employees, the current chairman, Michael Turner, muses on the principles that Fuller's has always possessed: 'I think the values that a family business has are really important for the staff who work here and the values have always been there. We look back to when people went to war and their jobs were kept open for them, their families were looked after, and when they got back they were re-employed and quite often housed in a company property.'

To celebrate the homecoming of their staff and the work of those who stayed during the dark years of the war, the company organised a day's cruise on the *Royal Eagle*, from Tower Bridge down to Southend for lunch and then back to London in the evening. On the official card commemorating the luncheon, the directors did feel it necessary to warn those attending that, 'It had been hoped to provide meals for everyone on board, but it is regretted that this is now impossible in view of the very limited facilities available. Everyone should, therefore, have a good breakfast before starting.' This was at a time, of course, when food was still being rationed. All was not lost, though, as the message also stated that 'liquid refreshments' would be available on board on both journeys.

A decade after drayhorse deliveries were consigned to history, the transport department continued to keep up with the times by moving tentatively into the age of the internal combustion engine. During 1946 the company bought four new Foden diesel lorries and trailers plus a Bedford lorry. This spelled the end for the ancient steam wagons. No longer could most of the maintenance work be carried out in the blacksmith's shop with hammer and forge. Instead, a more specialised transport garage was set up – though this was very small and nearly all repairs were done in the open air, regardless of the weather.

THE OLD WAYS: SOME OF THE LAST HORSE-DRAWN DRAYS TO BE USED; NOTE THE STEAM WAGON JUST VISIBLE TO THE LEFT

By the end of 1948 the 'steamers' had gone for good. Bernard Pearce, later to become transport service manager, when interviewed in the 1990s, recalled driving the last of the old wagons to its final resting place in a hedge in Amersham – though after many years this old faithful was rescued and restored and can be seen at rallies in the original Fuller's livery. Soon afterwards, the wine and spirit department purchased its first lorry. Owing to a shortage of new vehicles, this was an ex-War Department truck. 'It must have spent some time during the war in the desert,' Pearce remembered, 'because whenever we had to carry out repairs we kept finding sand.'

THIS WAS A TIME OF ECONOMIC STAGNATION. The brewing industry, like other manufacturing trades, took a long time to recover from the stresses of wartime, as well as the slump of the 1930s and post-war rationing. Expansion at the Griffin Brewery was slow and the company had neither the cash nor the inclination for any bold new enterprises. In 1946, brewers were commanded by the Labour government to restrict production to 85 per cent

LEWIS JOHN TURNER, FORMER MANAGING DIRECTOR AND CHAIRMAN

BETWEEN THE WARS, FULLER'S PRODUCED SOFT DRINKS, THOUGH THE ADVENT OF THE SECOND WORLD WAR SAW THEM CEASE UNTIL A LATER DALLIANCE WITH 7-UP

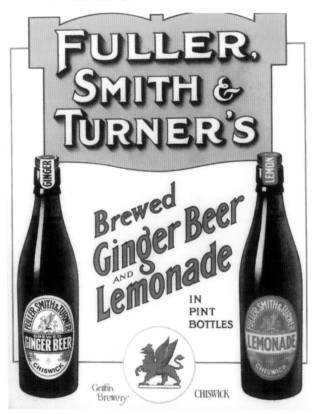

of the previous year; it was further reduced to 78 per cent in 1949. Beer still remained weak, while duty was high. Porter was no longer being brewed – Whitbread were the last company to make it before stopping in 1941. Mild was the most popular drink, especially with the working classes, with bitter seen as the beer of the bosses. In *The Brewer's Art* (published by Whitbread in 1948), the author postulated that there 'are four chief types of beer today: pale ale, mild ale, stout and Burton'. Fuller's would have brewed versions of all of these.

In line with other family breweries, Fuller's was keen on trying other ventures. A notable one in the early 1950s had nothing to do with beer at all. The directors were granted the franchise for manufacturing the American soft drink 7-Up, which involved importing a prepared syrup from the USA, then processing and bottling it. At first this was a great success – mostly because of the large numbers of US airmen still

# HOPS

BREWERS USE THE BITTERNESS AND FRAGRANCE OF THE HOP to balance the sweetness of the malt, but there's more to *Humulus lupulus*, or the 'wolf of the woods', than a mere sprinkling of brewing fairy dust. Hops yield resins and oils from a sticky yellow powder called lupulin, which is present in hop cones. These resins produce bitterness and have preservative qualities, while hop oils furnish flavour and aroma. Hence some hops are used for bitterness (kettle hops), while others are added later in the boil to provide their glorious aromas. Depending on the type used, hops can evoke aromas and flavours of passion fruit, grapefruit, pineapple, lychee, Seville orange (and even marmalade), cut grass, pine needles in a forest after a rain shower, resin, ripe peach or apricot skin, mint, melon and members of the allium family; the bitterness from the hop (courtesy of something called alpha acid, with some hops having more than others) can be as mellow or as assertive as the brewer needs it to be. Hop varieties in use at Fuller's include classic English ones such as Target, Challenger and Northdown (London Pride); Liberty and Goldings (Oliver's Island). Meanwhile, the US gets a look-in with Cascade, Liberty and Willamette (Wild River) – incidentally, the use of American hops is not new with Fuller's; a flick through the brewing logs before the First World War reveals the use of hops from Oregon for beers such as pale ale and AK.

# LONDON PRIDE FOR LIFE

9th June          60

CHFF/LG

Dear Mr. Tamman,

        May I send you my best congratulations for
being the first man ever to win a cask of beer for life.
It might call for some framed testimonial but I feel that
the photograph of the strong man with cask aloft will be
a more telling memorial - so long as you keep the secret!

        With regard to the future, who can tell what
it holds?   There may come a time when you would like to
have a cask but for the present, you tell me, you would
prefer the can.   I am therefore making arrangements for
you to be sent a case of canned LONDON PRIDE to celebrate  *as amnpd by*
the occasion (LONDON PRIDE in cans is a good deal stronger  *CHf*
that LONDON PRIDE on draught or in bottle), and we will
let you have three cases a year where ever you want them,
irrespective of where you may happen to reside in England.

        With best wishes.


                      Yours truly,

                         C.H.F.F.


                         Director,
              FULLER, SMITH & TURNER LTD.

TOWARDS THE END OF THE 1950S, Fuller's Brewery launched a billboard campaign that the company hoped would give it a more modern image. The poster featured the words 'Fuller's – London Pride' and showed a large, shiny vinyl single record. The purpose being to suggest, perhaps, that Fuller's was rock'n'roll and all that. Following on from this, Fuller's ran a competition that was aimed at finding the best poster for London Pride (the beer was launched in cask in 1959), with the prize being a cask of the eponymous beer every year for life plus a cheque for £50. According to the *Glasgow Herald* of 9 June 1960, 'after many false starts with guardsmen, London policemen and pearly kings and queens, the award was eventually won by a Frenchman with a study of the Oxford and Cambridge boat race, which the judges claimed captured the essence of London. The winner, Roger Tamman, a commercial artist now living in London, said that he likes beer when there is no wine.' Sadly, Roger Tamman died in 2015, but he did receive his regular cask of beer every year, though as a letter from the brewery to him from then director, Christopher Fuller, demonstrates, 'for the present, you tell me, you would prefer the can. I am therefore making arrangements for you to be sent a case of canned LONDON PRIDE to celebrate the occasion'.

serving in or near London. The 7-Up business, run by Gerald Turner (R.F.L. Turner's second son), was moved to a new factory on the site of the old maltings. But soon the Americans went home and a succession of wet summers did nothing for soft drinks sales. 7-Up, along with its factory, was eventually sold off to a producer of lemonade in 1965.

An altogether happier and more imaginative development took place in 1959, when Fuller, Smith & Turner formed a subsidiary company called the Griffin Catering Company. Led by Charles Williams, originally licensee of the Golden Lion in Hillingdon, this oversaw the brewery's managed houses. The enterprise was expanded still further by Lewis Turner,

**AN EARLY ADVERT FOR WHAT WOULD BECOME THE BREWERY'S FLAGSHIP BEER**

a future managing director and chairman, who went to the USA to study the way motels were run. His findings were put into practice in the early 1960s, when the Master Robert in Hounslow opened as the first of London's motels (the brewery was to sell it in 2000). Following Williams' untimely death in 1968, the task of running the catering company was successfully taken over by his son David, who not only continued to play a strong part in building up Griffin Catering as well as the managed house side of Fuller's, but also served as deputy chairman.

This was a straw in the wind. Pubs and the brewing industry were beginning to change and the speed of that change was about to accelerate with bewildering consequences. There were three contributing factors. One was catering: brewers were realising that if the public was going to be enticed into their pubs they must offer a wider range of food and more attractive surroundings. Fuller's, with its new subsidiary, was well placed to take advantage of the trend. The other two factors were more sinister, however. Giantism was sweeping every corner of British industry as the big conglomerates swallowed up their smaller rivals. And beer itself was on the verge of a major transformation that would change drinking habits and also galvanise a pressure group that would make the headlines with their campaigns. The traditional cask-conditioned product was under massive attack from a brash newcomer – keg beer.

Meanwhile, 25 April 1959, saw the launch of a very important beer from Fuller's. This beer was London Pride, which was available in cask for the first time. A beer of this name had been available in bottle for several years, but this cask beer, an adaptation of the brewery's Special Pale Ale with its roots in the beers of the late 19th century, would become one of the UK's most iconic beers.

# The Churchill Arms

SITTING ON A STREET CORNER IN THE MIDDLE OF KENSINGTON, the Georgian-built Churchill is one of London's most renowned (and award-winning) pubs. Originally opened in the 18th century, it was christened with its current name after the Second World War (a decision presumably influenced by the discovery that Winston Churchill's parents used to nip in for a quick one in the 19th century). Its current landlord, Gerry O'Brien, is a living legend. In 2015 he celebrated 30 years as manager of the Churchill and, under his sway, the pub has become renowned not only for its beers (it has been reckoned that, under his tenure so far, O'Brien has had two million pints of London Pride served), but for its colourful display of window boxes and hanging baskets on the exterior and an equally busy and dramatic collection of Churchill memorabilia and other bric-a-brac inside – there's a waterfall, for instance, with live fish swimming about at the base. As if that wasn't enough, the Churchill is also famous for its Thai restaurant– it was the first pub in London to do such a thing. Naturally, it's a popular pub and evenings can be made even more boisterous by the appearance of musicians, in one case a bagpipe-playing, kilt-wearing group over from Flanders. There's no such thing as an ordinary night at the Churchill.

THE CHURCHILL ARMS, 119 KENSINGTON CHURCH ST, LONDON W8 7LN

# TASTING NOTE

# LONDON PRIDE, 4.1% (4.7% BOTTLE)

THIS IS THE BEER that anyone who knows anything about beer thinks of whenever the name Fuller, Smith & Turner is mentioned. It's the flagship, the leader of the gang of exemplary beers emerging from the Griffin Brewery, a favourite in London and throughout the country, a beer that is about balance and drinkability. Fuller's first brewed a beer called London Pride in the middle of the 1950s, but it was only for bottling and its label declared it was a Special Pale Ale (it had its roots in the beers regularly produced from the late 19th century onwards). It was first produced as a cask-conditioned beer in 1959 and has since set off on its unique journey to be a beer that not only represents the best of Fuller's but the best of the city in which it is brewed.

The origins of its name? It refers to the hardy flower London Pride which flourished in the rubble left by the Blitz, and there has long been a story that the suggestion came from the winner of a competition held to name it at the end of the decade. However, Andrew Campbell's 1956 edition of *The Book of Beer* mentions bottled London Pride ('well-carbonated and slightly sweet'), so it probably was called after the flower and not the result of a naming competition. There was a competition for painting an inn sign for a pub to be named The London Pride, which took place in 1960.

There's a gleam of amber in the eye of the glass and a two-step groove of biscuit-like sweetness and deep orange citrus working out on the nose. A malt-derived sweetness combines adeptly with joyously deep orange on the palate, a hint of the kind of orange marmalade you spread on your morning toast perhaps, before a refreshingly bitter finish that lingers with the persistence of a peal of bells heard across a valley on a crisp autumnal morning.

# Frontier Battered Cod with Crispy Chips, Lemon, Tartare Sauce and Minted Peas

Serves 4

## INGREDIENTS

| | |
|---|---|
| 4 | 170–200g cod fillets |
| 2 | lemons, halved, to serve |

**For the tartare sauce:**

| | |
|---|---|
| 40g | baby capers, finely chopped |
| 40g | gherkins, finely chopped |
| 20g | finely chopped fresh dill |
| 1 | red onion, finely diced |
| juice and zest of 1 lemon | |
| 280g | mayonnaise |
| salt and ground white pepper | |

**For the crispy chips:**

| | |
|---|---|
| 1.5kg | potatoes (we use Potato Lovers), peeled and cut into chips |
| vegetable oil, for frying | |

**For the batter:**

| | |
|---|---|
| 920ml | Fuller's Frontier lager |
| 60g | fresh yeast |
| 500g | plain flour, plus extra for coating the cod |
| ½ tsp | salt |
| 1 tsp | black peppercorns |

**For the minted peas:**

| | |
|---|---|
| 230g | garden peas |
| 20g | unsalted butter |
| 5 | chopped mint leaves |

## METHOD

To prepare the tartare sauce, put the capers and gherkins in a bowl and add the dill and red onion. Add the lemon juice and zest, and the mayonnaise. Combine until well mixed, season to taste and set aside in the fridge until ready to use.

Blanch the chipped potatoes in a fryer set at 150°C for 5 minutes, then allow to cool.

Prepare the batter by gently warming the beer to blood temperature and whisk in the fresh yeast. Add the flour, salt and pepper and whisk until fully incorporated. Don't worry if there are any little lumps as they will crisp up during frying. Set aside.

To make crushed minted peas, blanch the peas for a minute in boiling water and place them straight into ice-cold water. Put the peas in a blender and pulse until crushed. Just before serving, heat the peas in a small pan with the butter and chopped mint, and season to taste.

Heat the fryer to 180°C and fry the chips again until crispy, then drain them and place in a bowl to keep warm. Season with salt.

Place the cod into seasoned flour and coat well, shaking off any excess flour. Place in the batter, then hold the cod up to allow any excess batter to drip off, then gently place the fish in the fryer at 180°C. Cook until golden and crispy (around 8 minutes), draining any oil from the fish by placing on to a clean J-cloth or kitchen roll. Season with salt and serve straightaway on a bed of crushed peas, with a good spoonful of tartare sauce and a portion of crispy chips served in a half pint glass or neatly on the plate. Garnish with half a lemon.

# CHAPTER SIX

# Cask Is Saved!

**LONDON PRIDE WAS LAUNCHED** at the end of the 1950s but this pristine pint would find itself in a very different world as the next decade moved on. London swung, the Beatles sang, students would revolt and England won the World Cup. In 1963, the future Labour prime minister, Harold Wilson, spoke of the 'white heat of technology', which would find its mirror image in the changes convulsing the British brewing industry. Breweries such as Whitbread and Bass became even bigger as smaller regional outfits were devoured and often closed while their beers were produced at the mother plant. Packaged beers, both in bottle and can, continued to increase in popularity, while lager began its great upward march through the institutions of British brewing. Names such as Skol, Harp and Carling became familiar sights on the British bar-top as a younger generation spurned the bitters and milds their fathers and grandfathers drank (many of them in their turn would eventually drink lager). This was also the decade when the beer style Burton vanished from breweries' portfolios – in 1969 Fuller's Old Burton Extra was replaced by the seasonal brew Winter Beer (this went on to become better known as ESB).

The licensed trade was also not immune to transformation as traditional pubs continued to be 'improved'. This usually meant turning a multi-roomed establishment into one big egalitarian bar, sometimes with a tacky theme. One brewing company allegedly drew up a plan for automatic beer-dispensing machines in some of its pubs. However, the change with the greatest potential for turning everything upside down was the emerging popularity of keg (or brewery-conditioned) beer in place of cask-conditioned.

Cask-conditioning gives a uniqueness to ale, where after being racked in a cask, the yeast continues to do its work during secondary conditioning in the pub cellar. The result, when treated correctly at the point of dispense and served at cellar temperature, is a beer with finesse and character. Unfortunately, if handled badly, it can also be unpredictable and unstable, and, more importantly, taste dreadful. Cask, or naturally conditioned beer, demands a certain expertise in storing and handling, and anecdotal evidence has suggested that this essential skill was lacking in many British pubs throughout the 1950s. In *Beer: The Story of the Pint,* Martyn Cornell stated that this unreliability led to the creation of many bottle and draught beer mixes, such as light and bitter, since a highly carbonated bottle of beer would liven up a half of flattish draught beer.

This kind of instability was (and is) not something cherished by many brewers – especially if a stable alternative is available. In brewing, the only alternative to cask-conditioned beer was bottled beer, but in May 1955 a new process had been perfected at Luton brewery J.W. Green (the product was actually called Flower's Keg, after the name of the Stratford-upon-Avon brewery Green had taken over), producing what was called 'bright' or keg beer. This was a beer that had been filtered and pasteurised to within an inch of its life and then served beneath a layer of carbon dioxide, which helped to keep it the same from the start to the finish. This meant it could last much longer than cask-conditioned beer. Here, surely, was the answer to a brewer's prayer.

Plenty of breweries had been on their knees and as a consequence praying hard since the war. Between

1946 and the late 1950s, beer consumption in Britain had dropped from 33 million to 25 million barrels a year. The introduction of death duties had also dealt a fatal blow to several family-run firms. Some went bankrupt; others gladly sold out to bigger companies, which is how the likes of Whitbread prospered.

Even though keg beer took on the sheen of a shining knight in armour, it did nothing to slow the attritional nature of the British brewing industry. On the contrary, by the early 1960s the new product was making it easier for big companies to succeed: keg beer was easy to transport over long distances, so it could be brewed in larger quantities at fewer sites throughout the country. Because there was no yeast in the cask, it did not have to settle prior to serving. In the late 1960s, the brewing industry was dominated by just seven giants: Bass, Allied, Whitbread, Watneys, Scottish & Newcastle, Courage and Guinness. They produced nearly 75 per cent of all British beers; the rest came from 104 smaller breweries such as Fuller's.

**FULLER'S, IT SEEMED,** would have to follow the crowd. Keg appeared unstoppable and the only way for a brewery to survive was to embrace it. A tank room for the new 'bright' beverage was installed at the Griffin Brewery, plus facilities for filtration and flash pasteurisation. Hand pumps were removed from the pubs and replaced with an electronic metering system, operated at the press of a button. Besides, the old plant was wearing out. Plans were made to phase out the production of cask-conditioned beer and brew nothing but keg. During this period, breweries such as Watneys installed tanks in their pub cellars, which were filled with a hosepipe from a tanker – Fuller's carried out experiments with this process and seriously thought about following the trend.

But the company's crisis went far deeper than that. Never had it been so near to closing down. In November 1968, the production director Lewis Turner drew up for the board a discussion document on the future of the brewery. He presented several options. The bleakest of these was to cease brewing entirely and simply operate managed and tenanted houses. The most optimistic option was to build a brand-new brewery on the site.

ANTONY ANSELL WITH THE REV JOHN YEEND AT THE OPENING OF THE SURVEYOR, WEST MOLESEY, IN 1974; ANSELL HIMSELF WENT INTO THE CHURCH A FEW YEARS LATER

**THE GRIFFIN BREWERY IN THE 1960S. NOTE THE PETROL STATION, WHICH HAS NOW BEEN DEMOLISHED**

Faced with these stark possibilities the directors, led by chairman Edward Fuller, were in no hurry to make a decision. Discussions meandered on over the next two years until at last, late in 1970, a compromise was reached: the brewery would be re-equipped on the existing site and there would be an increase in the production of bottled and bright beer. Plans were drawn up, costings prepared and planning permission sought, but there was still a delay.

Richard Fuller's view of this period was that 'the board couldn't make up its mind about whether to switch entirely to kegged beer. Had they done so I suspect we wouldn't be here today.'

So the months ticked by, but this hesitancy was to prove crucial. While the directors and planners argued and procrastinated, a growing consumer revolution was convulsing the brewing industry. In 1971, the Campaign for the Revitalisation of Ale (it changed its name to the snappier Campaign for Real Ale or CAMRA in 1973) was formed, with the aim of ensuring the survival of cask-conditioned beer as well as supporting smaller brewers such as Fuller's against the machinations of the big brewing companies. To many people's astonishment the campaign was spectacularly successful and by the end of 1973 there were 30,000 CAMRA members. Regional branches of the campaign held demonstrations against the closure of breweries. Meanwhile, its aims had dovetailed with the 1970s values of 'back to the land', as exemplified by John Seymour's best-selling book *The Complete Book of Self-Sufficiency*. This perfect storm helped to send sales of 'real ale' soaring and the products of the smaller independent breweries had become much treasured and sought-after.

Unsurprisingly, Fuller's took advantage of this shift in public taste, thanks largely to the charm and energy of sales director Antony Ansell (who, with former chairman Anthony Fuller and one-time company secretary Ian Turner, had become a director in 1968). The son of Sir Michael Ansell and Victoria Fuller, he devoted a good deal of effort to wooing the campaigners.

# BREWING PROCESS

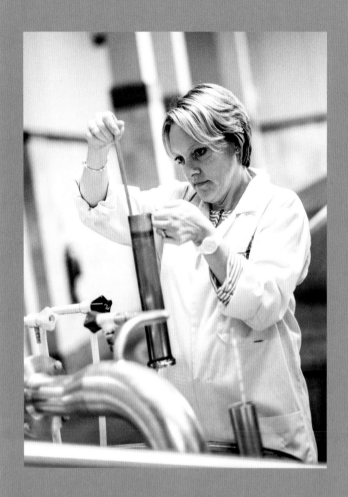

**BREWING STARTS WITH THE MASH,** when ground malted barley is mixed (or mashed) in with hot water, which is then maintained at a set temperature over a period of time. The liquid that drains away into the copper is called the wort, a sugar-rich concoction that is then boiled. The first addition of hops comes at the beginning and these will be the varieties that contain the most alpha acids – these hops are used for bitterness. Hops are then added during the middle of the boil and at the end – these will be the aroma hops, which if thrown in at the start would see their gorgeous aromatic qualities boiled away. At Fuller's, the hopped wort is then cooled and sent to fermenting vessels where yeast is added. The temperature rises to 20°C and the yeast starts to turn sugar into alcohol. After half the sugar is fermented the beer is reduced to 17°C, and after another three to four days one-fifth of the sugar is left. During a further three to four days, the beer is cooled down to 6°C and the alcohol is checked to make sure it's reached the correct level. Yeast is then removed (some of it will be used in the production of Marmite) and the beer makes its way to the maturation tanks where it will develop a depth of flavour over time, after which it will be racked into casks or bottled and finally delivered to the drinker.

He listened attentively to their views and made sure they were invited to pub openings and other brewery events. As a result, Fuller's became strongly identified with the real ale revolution. In 1992, Anthony Fuller recognised this when writing in a book celebrating CAMRA's 21st anniversary: 'The emergence of CAMRA was the point that started to change the real ale brewers' fortunes.'

**BY ANOTHER LUCKY COINCIDENCE** Fuller's introduced ESB, or Extra Special Bitter, in 1971, a potent beer that struck a resonant chord with beer drinkers (there were not many strong beers available at this time). As well as being one of the strongest regularly brewed draught beers in the country (at 5.5%), it was also one of the tastiest. With ESB, Fuller's brewing team not only produced an excellent ale, but they also created a whole new beer category – extra special bitter (based on Fuller's ESB) remains a beer style that is especially popular with today's American craft brewers. As ESB grew in popularity it won CAMRA's first Champion Beer of Britain competition in 1978. It then went on to repeat this success in 1981 and 1985, while London Pride won the accolade in 1979 and Chiswick Bitter in 1989. Anthony Fuller recalls that, 'Gerald Turner [father of Michael] played a great role in encouraging tenants to stock and sell ESB – he was often quite "jolly" when he came back from lunch.'

There was a third stroke of luck. During the late 1950s, the Cromwell Road extension had connected west London with the Great West Road. A major artery, the A4 and (later) the link with the M4 passed right in front of the brewery gates. To countless thousands of motorists, the premises of Fuller, Smith & Turner became a prominent landmark and the brewery's name one of the most familiar in London. The publicity was worth a thousand advertising campaigns.

By 1974, circumstances had changed dramatically. Sales of bottled and keg beers had slowed considerably, while those of draught beer had rocketed. The market for a brewery of Fuller's size and range had been transformed and the company had to take advantage of this – rapidly. Lewis Turner, the new chairman, realised that greater efficiency was sorely needed in many areas, notably financial matters, which had never been one of the brewery's strong points. He brought in a West End auditor called Noel Chambers to overhaul

the company's accounting methods. Chambers was an inspired choice. Shrewd, hard-working, yet diffident, he eased the erratic cash flow by ensuring that invoices were sent off promptly and regularly, and drew up a new programme of investments and loans.

As Richard Fuller remarks, 'We had a new generation coming in during the 1970s replacing my father's generation. My father was relatively old, he had been one of the originals in the 1920s, and had seen it through from that time. This period saw the introduction of new blood – in the form of Lewis Turner and then Anthony Fuller.'

Sales – and profits – looked rosier by the month; beer sales increased rapidly for two consecutive years, the profits from which gave Fuller's the cash to start redeveloping the brewery. Having taken a long time to

**DOWN WITH THE OLD, UP WITH THE NEW. THE BUILDING PROGRAMME WHICH BEGAN IN 1975 TOOK SIX YEARS TO COMPLETE. (LEFT) THE OLD BRICK CHIMNEY IS DEMOLISHED. (BELOW) A MATURATION TANK IS SWUNG INTO POSITION OVER THE ROOFTOPS**

# BREWING STYLES
# LAGER

LAGER HAS BEEN BREWED IN LONDON SINCE 1881, when the Austro-Bavarian Brewery was founded in Tottenham. Until the 1960s it was a rare beast, although in 1932 the *Brewers' Guardian* noted that annual sales of Graham's Golden Lager (which was later renamed Skol) had increased over five years from three to 13 million half-pints. A note of caution should be sounded, though: in an answer to a parliamentary question, *Hansard* recorded that 4,891,104,000 pints of beer were brewed in July 1931. From the 1960s, the likes of Carling Black Label, Skol and Harp were staples at the bar-top, which was why family brewers tried to brew their own. Looking back, many of these lagers have not come down through history with their reputations intact, especially when compared to the classic Pilsners, Helles, Bocks and Dunkels of Germany and the Czech Republic.

When Fuller's released K2 in the 1980s they were only doing what a lot of family brewers were doing at the same time: producing a lager for their pub estate. They went against the contemporary trend by avoiding the kind of fake Germanic name that was common with other breweries, such as Einhorn (brewed in Salford), Langdorf (Rutland) and Konig Lager (Dorset). However, K2 was an unfortunate name given the climbing disaster on the eponymous mountain in 1986; Fuller's was a major sponsor of the expedition, and brewing of the beer stopped soon afterwards.

As for the science and the difference between lager and ale? The fermentation process for lager differs from that of ale in that the yeast works at a much cooler temperature. It has always been called bottom fermentation, though as the yeast works its way throughout the whole of the fermenting liquid it would be more correct to call it cold-fermentation. Once the first fermentation is completed, lager beers are put into conditioning vessels (or lagering tanks), where a full attenuation can take place over a few weeks, though a lot of cost-conscious companies used to cut that time (not so Fuller's, whose Frontier Craft Lager is conditioned for 42 days). Attenuation is a process whereby nearly all the malt sugars left are turned into carbon dioxide and alcohol, giving the lager a smooth, soft character.

make the original decision, the directors were now in the happy position of being able to change their minds about the redevelopment of the plant. Out went the scheme for extending the bright beer production. The space would be used for extra storage of draught beer.

The new master plan involved several stages. Phase one, started in 1975, was the most modest, extending the capacity for fermentation, with the installation of 11 conical vessels. This posed a fresh brewing problem. Unlike the old 'open squares', which used top fermenting yeast, they required a yeast strain that settled on the bottom; at the time, brewers believed that cask-conditioned beer could not be made with conicals. After a series of trials, a suitable yeast strain was propagated from the original Fuller's yeast, enabling brewing to continue with the minimum of disturbance to the original process. A chilling plane and two gas and oil fired boilers were also added, with a new steel chimney replacing the old brick one, which had been a Chiswick landmark for over half a century.

Richard Fuller once more: 'We were brewing good beer and our visionary head brewer, Reg Drury, persuaded the board to invest in a new brewhouse and also to swap our open squares for conicals. This was a time of massive investment in the brewery that set the culture of the business, which is that we are always going to invest in quality.'

Chairman Michael Turner also recalls the period as one of shrewd investment and foresight: 'Reg and my uncle [Lewis Turner] started redeveloping the brewing, brought in conicals and brewed alongside the open squares, all of which enabled us to start a new regime and keep the beer free from infection. Once Anthony Fuller became managing director in 1975 he also made sure that we started to invest in good pubs.'

Phase two was much more ambitious. It required major changes to the brewery site, and thus prolonged attention from the planning authorities. Permission was at last granted in July 1978 – almost exactly ten years after Lewis Turner had presented his original document.

By 1980, the new malt storage tower had been completed. Standing 20 metres high, it was equipped with machinery for handling malt in bulk from lorries and storing it in four huge silos, each holding 30 tonnes. That April, the new warehouse complex was opened. Covering 4,200 square metres, it was the focus of the new distribution system. Full casks and kegs were stored here, ready for loading on to the

**AS WELL AS FEEDING SPENT YEAST TO PIGS, FULLER'S SEND SOME TO THE MARMITE FACTORY IN BURTON-ON-TRENT, WHERE IT IS USED IN THE MANUFACTURE OF THIS ICONIC, LOVE-IT-OR-HATE-IT SPREAD**

drays, while empty casks were unloaded. The steel floor was covered with thick rubber to muffle the noise and prevent damage to the casks. The area also housed offices, the cask-washing and racking plant and a keg-racking plant for the expanding lager market.

A year later the old racking room was converted into a fermentation and tank room. A giant crane swung six conical fermenting vessels high over the rooftops and lowered them into place; they were soon flanked by 12 maturation vessels.

The new facilities were proudly opened on 28 April 1981. By now, Fuller's not only had a new managing director (Anthony Fuller), but also a financial position of impressive and growing strength. Pre-tax profits had climbed above £1 million in 1977 for the first time in the company's history and sales of draught beer had significantly increased. Profits went on to reach £2 million in 1982, £3 million in 1984 and a staggering £5 million in 1986.

Meanwhile, the next phase of the redevelopment was hurrying ahead, though not without difficulties. The

new brewhouse had to be built within very cramped confines, bordered by four existing buildings, one of which was listed. And all the while full production had to carry on around the construction works. New chilled and hot liquor tanks were manoeuvred into place, followed by two wort-boiling coppers. Lorries brought the latter from Burton-on-Trent (one of which took a wrong turning and got stuck under a bridge). Local MP Barney Hayhoe officially opened the brewhouse in September 1986.

The new plant not only improved the brewery's capacity but also gave Fuller's the ability to brew lager for the first time. As has been noted, lager, or rather the British version of it, had been growing in popularity since the 1960s and been boosted by aggressive publicity campaigns on TV and in the press, as well as a series of hot summers where lager offered a refreshing alternative. For several years the company had bought in Harp lager to sell in its pubs and off-licences. Even with the boom in draught beer, lager had steadily advanced until by 1986 it accounted for 29 per cent of Fuller's total sales. In line with many other family breweries (including south London competitor Young's), the time had come for the company to brew its own brand.

A trial lager went on sale in selected pubs during that summer. Those who tried it were enthusiastic about what they tasted, but then there was the question of what it should be called. Inspiration came in rather a bizarre fashion, when a letter arrived asking for sponsorship on behalf of an expedition that was setting out to climb K2, the second highest mountain in the world. Sponsorship was given and Fuller's K2 lager was born. Its launch, however, was clouded by tragedy following the death of two climbers on their way down from the mountain's summit. It was not a good omen.

TWENTY YEARS BEFORE, Fuller's had been a struggling local brewery. Now, vast new horizons seemed to be opening up on every side. Bottled ESB Export was being shipped to the USA, where it was sold in pockets over a huge area, stretching from Los Angeles and San Francisco to Denver and New York.

# KEG VS CASK

**DURING THE 1970S THE KEG–CASK DIVIDE** was very simple. Keg beers were filtered and pasteurised, kept under, and dispensed by, gas and served ice-cold. It was easy to look after and serve and part of its popularity was that the drinker knew what to expect. However, as the *Sunday Mirror* demonstrated in a special report in 1971, a lot of these beers were exceedingly weak. 'Chemical fizz' was one of the milder insults thrown in its direction by fans of cask-conditioning, emboldened by the success of the Campaign for Real Ale. As for cask beer, this was seen as 'live', as the beer had yeast still working away in the cask in the pub cellar, or secondary fermentation as it is better known. This process, in the eyes of a growing group of drinkers, gave cask beer character, taste, a freshness, a gentle carbonation and a chance for the hops and malt to show their strengths. Cask beer has continued to grow in popularity but contemporary keg beer, as produced by Fuller's and a host of smaller 'craft' brewers, is a much more flavoursome beast and has proved popular, especially with younger drinkers and even cask beer lovers looking for something different. The old battle lines of cask vs keg have faded away and beer drinkers are all the richer for the choice they have.

When the British Virgin Islands staged a beer festival in 1987, London Pride was the only 'real' draught beer. In July 1990, a deal was signed with the Dutch-based brewery Grolsch, who were eager to import and sell Fuller's beer across the whole of the USA. At the same time, Fuller's pubs began stocking Grolsch's draught lager.

Developments at home were even more exhilarating. This was partly (and surprisingly) due to the 1989 report on the brewing industry by the Monopolies and Mergers Commission (MMC). The MMC inquiry had been instigated a couple of years before and the Brewers' Society had set up a steering committee, one of whose members was Anthony Fuller, who was

then chairman of the society. The Beer Orders which followed the report stated that all breweries with more than 2,000 pubs had to sell or free from the tie 50 per cent of the excess over 2,000. They also permitted the tenants of those breweries to buy one guest cask-conditioned ale from someone other than their own brewery, which was an enormous benefit for a brewery such as Fuller's. As Fuller was to say later when talking to *The Publican*, 'The Beer Orders completely changed the face of the pub industry.'

The MMC's report and the Beer Orders were bitterly criticised and in some cases damaged trade, with many pubs being forced to close. Yet they brought immense benefits to expanding, medium-sized

# PERSONAL PROFILE
# ANTHONY FULLER C.B.E.

ANTHONY FULLER JOINED THE BREWERY as a management trainee in 1963, but not before he'd spent over three years in the Guards and then a further 18 months travelling around the world. It had been made very clear to him by his father that he would eventually join the brewery. In an interview given to the CAMRA newspaper *What's Brewing* to mark his retirement as executive chairman in 2002, he said, 'My father told me my future lay in the brewery and I was never given the opportunity to do anything else.' However, he did manage to make the most of his gap year-and-a-half, visiting the USA, Canada, Australia, Japan and Hong Kong, but then his father left him in no doubt that it was time to come home. 'The telegrams started chasing me. I was called back just at the point I'd really started enjoying myself.'

By 1975 Fuller was the brewery's estates director and, interviewed in *The Publican* in 2005, he recalled that this 'was a difficult time as we were considering our future in the light of the creation of CAMRA. We were on the verge of moving out to Heathrow, building a new brewery and focusing on keg bitter – thankfully, and mainly due to the property crash of 1973–74, we decided against it.' It was a close-run thing as the brewery nearly got planning permission to redevelop its site for a hotel, offices and residential buildings from the loading dock down to the river. He had also focused on this theme in *What's Brewing* in 2002, saying, 'There was a property boom and our site was very valuable. It would have been efficient but we would have lost all our charm.' Thankfully for London, Fuller's stayed put and the resurgence of cask-conditioned beer helped them survive.

Fuller was appointed executive chairman in 1982 and stayed in that role for 20 years. During this period he oversaw the growth of the company and from 1986 to 1989 he was also chairman of the Brewers' Society, when the Monopolies and Mergers Commission took submissions on the future of the brewing industry. By all accounts his role was crucial (it was usual for brewers the size of Fuller's only to serve as chairman for one year but during the MMC inquiry he did three, for which he was awarded the CBE). When he stepped down in 2002 and Michael Turner took over the role of executive chairman, he was quoted as saying: 'During my time as chairman of Fuller's I have witnessed many changes in the industry. Sadly, today there are far fewer independent regional brewers than there were 20 years ago. To be successful we have had to constantly evolve and challenge all that we do, while staying true to our underlying principles of Quality, Service and Pride. I have worked with Michael for over ten years and am delighted to hand over the reins to an individual who constantly strives for excellence and who I know will continue to build on the company's strengths.'

Anthony Fuller remained as non-executive chairman from 2002 to 2007 and then spent another three years on the board as non-executive director before retiring. He left a great legacy and many fond memories among both staff and those in the wider industry who worked with him. As he said in his *What's Brewing* interview, 'It's been great fun.'

**A SYMPHONY IN STAINLESS STEEL: MASH TUNS IN THE BREWERY**

companies such as Fuller, Smith & Turner. When the big brewers put their excess pubs on the market, Fuller's were on hand to snap up the best of them. In the autumn of 1990, they surprised the brewing world by purchasing no fewer than 44 outlets from Ind Coope, the pub division of Allied Breweries, a move that Richard Fuller recalls as 'a big deal for us, very important'. Most of them lay in a swathe extending across Buckinghamshire and Oxfordshire to the edge of the Cotswolds, giving the brewery a well-defined new sphere of influence. Fuller's products would now be directly distributed over a significantly larger area, bordered by the Cotswold Hills, Docklands, Luton and Basingstoke.

**THE BREWERY'S INTERESTS** had been growing in another direction all this while. Off-licences had played an increasingly important part in its trade, largely through the inspired efforts of Christopher Fuller (his sure-fire way of expanding the number of outlets was to confront fellow directors with his recommendation for a new one on a Friday afternoon, when they were

anxious to get away for the weekend and happy to agree to anything; by the time he retired there were 60 of them), but a growing public taste for wine had produced a demand for something more than the old-fashioned bottle shops. Accordingly, the company off-licences began to be transformed into genuine wine merchants; in some cases, over half of the selling space was devoted to wine for the first time. Michael Turner, who joined the company in 1978, began his career in this area: 'I joined on 12 June, after having qualified as a chartered accountant. I worked on the wine side and at first was an understudy to Anthony Fuller, who was in charge of wine, and then after a couple of years I took over from him when he became the chairman.'

The effect of this hard work with the wine was dramatic. Within a few years, Fuller's shops had become highly respected not only by customers, but also by wine writers and other members of the trade. This respect brought in a brace of major awards with Fuller's being voted Regional Wine Merchant of the Year by both *Wine Magazine* and the *Sunday Telegraph* in the early 1990s.

The K2 venture came to an end in 1992. There was simply not enough room for storing the lager during its long fermentation and maturation process. Besides which, Fuller's had proved that their real strength lay in brewing traditional English draught ale, something which had earned them an abiding reputation: especially as their products were most widely available as guests up and down the land. As Michael Turner recalls, 'We were very lucky when the Beer Orders came along – we had K2 and the big brewers wanted London Pride and we were able to stop brewing K2 and use the lager farm to ferment London Pride in. We could get twice as much ale through it, and then took Carling when it was the best-selling lager in the country. You would assume lager volumes would shoot up, but they dropped. Both Whitbread and Bass were selling and distributing London Pride and we advertised it. London Pride was very easy to look after and had, and still has, a reputation for dropping bright quickly.'

**AROUND THE SAME TIME,** the company took a step forward with its pubs and launched the Ale & Pie initiative; the concept was developed in prime city centre sites and aimed to appeal to a clientele aged 25–45 and in the business sector. The idea was that each pub would be named after a pie and the first in the series was the Stargazey in Fulham, in 1992 (the stargazey pie features pilchards sticking their heads out of the pastry). However, with the opening of the former Bank of England in 1994 as the Old Bank of England, this pie-only naming rule was broken. 'When we bought the former Bank of England in the City,' said a spokesman at the time, 'we couldn't think of calling it anything other than the Old Bank of England. But we do have a special pie in each pub – for instance, the sausage and bacon pie in the Jack Horner and the Melton Mowbray pie in the Melton Mowbray.' The practice of specialising in pie-making has continued: each pub makes its own fresh pies on a daily basis.

In 1997, the brewery bought the Counting House, an eight-storey former bank in Cornhill in the City, and then fitted it out at a cost of £3.5 million. Much of the original interior, such as the mosaic floor and

THE QUEEN MOTHER PULLS A PINT OF ESB AT THE SALUTATION IN HAMMERSMITH IN 1989, WITH ANTHONY FULLER WATCHING ON THE LEFT

THE FLOOR OF THE OLD MASH TUN, NOW PROUDLY DISPLAYED IN THE FULLER'S HOCK CELLAR, IN WHICH FOR OVER A CENTURY, A DYNASTY OF BEERS, INCLUDING LONDON PRIDE AND ESB, BEGAN THEIR JOURNEY

marble walls, was sympathetically restored. There are currently 15 Ale & Pie pubs, including the Old Joint Stock in Birmingham, which is the only one outside the South East. The idea has clearly taken off and been a great success (though the Stargazey is no longer with the company).

The Griffin premises were now looking like a building site, as the fourth and final stage of the rebuilding and re-equipping neared its end. The new brewhouse was finally completed in January 1995. The old mash tuns, marked as dating from the early 19th century, were replaced with new and larger ones, allowing a much-needed increase in capacity. These were installed on the same floor level as the coppers, making it necessary to raise the roof height by four metres. Most of the external walls were clad with reclaimed brick to match the existing buildings.

**THE 150TH ANNIVERSARY** of Fuller, Smith & Turner was celebrated with a very special beer: 1845. This

was the creation of head brewer, Reg Drury, and was the brewery's first bottle-conditioned beer for many years. The Prince of Wales came to the brewery to start the mash and add the hops for the debut brew of the beer, such was the importance of this anniversary. 1845 also broke new ground in that Drury used amber malt, which featured a lot in the Victorian era, for colour and flavour.

According to the current head brewer, John Keeling, who joined the company in 1981, 'We started producing beers that were different to our core range back in the 1990s with Mr Harry, which was then followed up by 1845 – it has had a slow momentum but we have gone from having no new product development programme to a pretty healthy and lively one. However, they all should make money, they are not vanity products. 1845 was only intended to be brewed in 1995 and was based on an old recipe from 1845. It is matured for 100 days and has a shelf life of two years.'

RAISING A GLASS TO SUCCESS: THEN HEAD BREWER REG DRURY (*CENTRE, WEARING TIE*) AND THE TEAM, INCLUDING HIS EVENTUAL SUCCESSOR JOHN KEELING (*FAR LEFT*)

The beer has won many awards since its debut and is a regular in bottle and often appears in cask. You could argue that its development by Reg Drury was just one of the many steps the late head brewer (he died in 2015) took to help make Fuller's the force it is today. According to John Keeling, who was made head brewer on Drury's recommendation when he retired in 1999, 'to the junior brewers Reg was like a schoolmaster; in fact the beer writer Michael Jackson described him as your favourite Latin master. He was very patient and didn't hand out many tellings-off. Equally rare was getting high praise – he would allow you to make mistakes and when you made one the feeling was "what can we do to stop this happening again?" The biggest thing he did for Fuller's was the drive for quality, such as overseeing buying the plant that delivered the high quality. His era saw the drive for quality and consistency – that was a big part of his legacy.'

In 150 years the partnership of three families had brought a brewing dynasty to life and survived quarrels, world wars, brewing trends and many other changes and challenges. The birthday was celebrated and then it was time to move into the future.

FULLER'S CURRENT HEAD BREWER, JOHN KEELING

# FULLER'S PUB PROFILE
## The Star Tavern

**THE STAR IS A SURVIVOR.** Originally built towards the end of the 18th century when it housed the servants of the local aristocracy, it has lived through several ages of London pub life: the beer shops of the 1830s, the glitz and glass of the gin palace, the Defence of the Realm Act during the First World War, the 'Brewers' Tudor' architectural craze between the wars, the destruction of the Blitz and the changes that wrought such damage in traditional pubs in the 1960s and 1970s. It has prevailed. Inside, there are three separate areas: the bar, an adjoining lounge and a back room, all of which feature old prints and handbills on the wall. The feel of the pub is that it has settled into its age with great ease. It's a pub that is quietly confident. The best time to enjoy it is in the afternoon, between the lunchtime rush and evening hordes, when there's the quiet buzz of conversation and you get a sense of an oasis in the centre of diplomatic London. In beery circles, the Star is famous for having been in the *Good Beer Guide* for over 40 years, but there's also a hint of infamy attached to the pub. It had a racy reputation during the 1950s and 1960s and was popular with both high and low life, while model and showgirl Christine Keeler reputedly met her politician lover John Profumo above the pub. Then there was the caper. Sometime in 1963, in a private room guarded by a doorman, the gang that would become known as the Great Train Robbers got together to plan their heist. The Star continues to survive, the gang didn't.

THE STAR TAVERN, 6 BELGRAVE MEWS WEST, LONDON SW1X 8HT

# TASTING NOTE
## ESB, 5.5%

**AN ENTRY IN A FULLER'S BREWING LOGBOOK** from Wednesday, 10 February 1971 reveals that one of the beers being brewed on this day is ESB. Could this be the first brew of the beer that was launched in 1971, even though it had been first produced as a seasonal two years earlier under the name of Winter Beer? Whether it was or not, we do know that Fuller's ESB went on to take the drinking world by storm, especially as its strength was rare for a regular beer at the time. The beer was also notable in that extra special bitter has become an identifiable style, especially in the USA – the classification usually means a beer that is stronger than a bitter, and full of hop character though nothing like an India pale ale. According to current head brewer John Keeling, ESB was the first Fuller's beer he drank: 'Me and a couple of mates came to London from Manchester to see Frank Zappa in concert sometime in the 1970s and we went into a Fuller's pub and asked the landlord what we should drink. He suggested ESB and we had several pints before going to the concert.'

Burnished bronze in colour, this has a rich nose of Seville orange with a biscuit-like graininess in the background. On the palate there is more citrus and also a tangy marmalade note alongside a rich malt character. It's full-bodied and powerful, though very easy to drink. The finish is bittersweet and lasting.

# PERFECT WITH FULLER'S ESB

# Warm Chocolate Brownie with Chocolate Crumb, Earl Grey Ice Cream and Chocolate Sauce

Serves 8

## INGREDIENTS

### For the chocolate brownie:

| | |
|---|---|
| 300g | white flour |
| 1 tsp | baking powder |
| 225g | cocoa powder |
| 400g | dark chocolate |
| 500g | unsalted butter |
| 750g | caster sugar |
| 9 | eggs |
| 400g | white chocolate chips |

### For the chocolate crumb:

| | |
|---|---|
| 30g | unsalted butter |
| 50g | Callebaut dark chocolate, broken into pieces |
| 40g | cocoa powder |
| 60g | caster sugar |
| 30g | plain flour |

### For the chocolate sauce:

| | |
|---|---|
| 125ml | water |
| 125g | caster sugar |
| 120g | Callebaut dark chocolate, broken into pieces |
| 40g | cocoa powder |

### To serve:

Earl Grey ice cream (or similar)

## METHOD

First make the chocolate crumb. Preheat the oven to 160°C/fan oven 140°/gas mark 3. Place the butter and the chocolate pieces in a bowl and set over a pan of simmering water so that the chocolate and butter melt together. Meanwhile, weigh out the dry ingredients into a bowl. Pour the melted butter and chocolate into the dry ingredients and combine well until the mixture becomes a paste. Spread on to a baking tray lined with greaseproof paper and cook in the preheated oven for 4 minutes. Remove the tray from the oven and use a fork or spoon to stir the mixture round – this will help make sure it cooks evenly. Bake for a further 4 minutes and repeat the mixing process. Bake again for a final 4 minutes. Once cooled, the mixture will be ready to break into crumbs.

For the chocolate brownie, line a 20cm square baking tin with greaseproof paper and turn the oven up to 200°C/fan oven 180°C/gas mark 6. In a bowl, sift together the flour, baking powder and cocoa powder. Melt the dark chocolate and butter in a bain-marie – allow to cool slightly. Mix together the sugar and eggs until they are at the ribbon stage, then fold in the chocolate mixture, followed by the dry ingredients. Lastly, fold in the white chocolate chips. Pour the brownie mixture into the prepared tin and bake for 14 minutes. Allow to cool in the tin before removing and cutting into squares or oblongs.

Meanwhile, make the chocolate sauce. Heat the water and sugar together in a heavy-based saucepan until the sugar has dissolved and the mixture has come to a simmer. Place the chocolate pieces and cocoa powder in a bowl and pour over the hot water and sugar mixture. Whisk until all the chocolate has melted and you have a shiny chocolate mixture.

To serve, warm the brownies either in the oven at 180°C/fan oven 160°C/gas mark 4 for a few minutes or in the microwave for 10 seconds. Spread some chocolate sauce on each plate and top with a sprinkling of chocolate crumb and a warm brownie. Finish with a little more of the chocolate crumb on top and serve with a scoop of Earl Grey ice cream.

# FULLER'S PUB PROFILE
# The Bat & Ball

**YOU DON'T HAVE TO CARRY A COPY OF *WISDEN*** in your coat pocket to guess which game the name of this cosy country pub is most linked with. Yes, it's cricket, the game that defines the English summer, but it's not just any old cricket – this venerable brick and flint building stands directly opposite Broadhalfpenny Down, a cricket field where the rules of the modern game were first defined in the 18th century. The Bat & Ball was once called the Broadhalfpenny Hut (or just the Hutt, according to some sources), but in all likelihood had its name changed during those thrilling times when a local team would often play against an England XI and occasionally win (and then all the team would repair back to the pub for refreshment). Naturally the interior is chock-a-block with all manner of cricketing memorabilia, but this wasn't always the case. At one stage, Allied Breweries ran the place and dispensed with all the mementoes; they also renamed it the Natterjack, as if to add insult to injury. Thankfully, the locals held on to these precious relics and when Gales bought the pub and changed it back they were able to return them to their rightful home. Even if cricket leaves you cold, there can be no better place to find yourself on a summer's evening, a glass of bittersweet HSD in hand, with the thwack of leather on willow cannonading across the field as a lone batsman elegantly defies a fast bowler.

THE BAT & BALL, HYDEN FARM LANE, WATERLOOVILLE, HAMPSHIRE PO8 0UB

# CHAPTER SEVEN

# Challenges And Opportunities

**AFTER THE 150TH BIRTHDAY CELEBRATIONS** it was back to work and, apart from the day-to-day considerations of selling beer and enticing people into pubs, there was plenty of activity in the brewing world in 1995. For a start, family brewers such as Fuller's had woken up to the problems caused by the flood of cheap beers being smuggled across the Channel. This phenomenon was a perfect storm combining the high rate of duty on British beers and the opening of the Channel Tunnel in 1994. These two factors allowed people the chance of a quick shopping trip over to Calais, where a group of specially opened warehouses were stacked to the ceilings with cases of cheap bottled beer. This was not good for the pub trade.

'This is the biggest threat to London's pubs since the Luftwaffe,' was Anthony Fuller's response when speaking at a London Brewers Association seminar in 1995, which was held to publicise the growing threat from cheap continental liquor, according to a report in CAMRA's *What's Brewing*. Fuller's colleague, Stuart Neame, then vice-chairman of Shepherd Neame, also spoke: 'In 1990 we were the market leader in Kent. Today we are in second place. But we have not lost to Whitbread or Courage, but to a small brewery just outside St Omer.' These imports would be a constant thorn in the side of British breweries throughout the rest of the decade and well into the next millennium.

The period from the mid-1990s onwards was generally a tough time for cask-conditioned beer; many breweries were bought up and closed and cask beer sales fell. However, Fuller's bucked this downward trend – in 1997, the company reported a 5 per cent rise in the sale

of cask beers. Meanwhile, sales of London Pride hit the 100,000-barrel mark, while ESB had a 20 per cent rise in sales. In 1999, more good news came when it was reported that Fuller's share of the cask beer market had risen from 2.6 per cent to 3.1, with London Pride increasing its sales by 6 per cent. This was all a sign of good management under the chairmanship of Anthony Fuller and equally excellent brewing being orchestrated by head brewer, Reg Drury.

Another problem facing cask beer brewers was the runaway success of what was called nitro-keg (or smoothflow) – creamy, nitrogen-filled, brewery-conditioned beers that ate into the market for cask. Even Fuller's launched one briefly in 1996; it was called London Cream and aimed at Guinness and lager drinkers, though it didn't last too long.

On the publicity front, April 1997 saw a new departure for the company, when an advert for London Pride was aired on national television for the first time. This was also the first use of the familiar campaign strapline 'Whatever You Do, Take Pride'. The campaign continued and, three years later, Fuller's invested £1.5 million in a new TV campaign, which was overseen by Mark Mylod, better known for his work as director of the BBC's *The Royle Family*. According to a report in *What's Brewing*, 'The advertising is aimed squarely at the heart of keg and lager territory – in Fuller's words, "those who might normally reject traditional ale". It broke in April and will be repeated during summer's Euro 2000 football extravaganza and in the autumn.' This link-up with TV advertising would eventually lead to the involvement of former *Top Gear* presenter James May in 2010.

On the brewing floor, too, 1997 was a special year as it saw the release of the first ever Vintage Ale, a bottle-conditioned beer that is now brewed annually. The success of 1845 emboldened Reg Drury to create more special beers. 'Reg and I wanted to create a truly outstanding beer,' recalled John Keeling in 2006 at a tasting of ten vintages from 1997 onwards. 'This was not about volume, it was about producing a one-off Vintage Ale. At the time we didn't know how successful the beer would be. We certainly didn't know that one day we would have an evening like this.'

**1997 SAW THE FIRST VINTAGE ALE, WHOSE ANNUAL LAUNCH IS AWAITED WITH KEEN ANTICIPATION BY BEER LOVERS**

The Vintage Ales have gone on to become one of the most eagerly awaited releases in the beer connoisseur's calendar, especially as they change and develop over time. Reg Drury, who was also at the 2006 tasting, said that a shelf life of three years was put on the bottle, but '10 to 15 would be about right'.

There was a lot of positive action in Fuller's pub and bars sector as well. In 1998 the Churchill Arms was awarded *Evening Standard* Pub of the Year. This was a well-deserved triumph for its ebullient licensee Gerry O'Brien, who celebrated his 30th year at this iconic Kensington pub in 2015. The following year saw the launch of the Fine Line chain of bars, whose interiors featured a comforting selection of soft furnishings and emphasised wine rather than beer. At the time, there was a general feeling in the beer and brewing industry that pubs were too masculine; there was a need for venues that were more attractive to women – the All Bar One chain, which opened its first outlet in 1994, had become a success and other breweries and pub companies felt they could follow their own path in appealing to women. Fine Line was an immediate success and the concept won Best Newcomer at the Retailer's Retailer of the Year awards. At the same time, three pubs in Reading, Portsmouth and Slough were rebranded as Broadwalk, with a focus on food. However, these were sold off in 2002.

Wine had always been important to Fuller's. Michael Turner had worked on the wine side of the business when he first joined in 1978, as an understudy to Anthony Fuller. Then there was its award-winning Quality Wine Merchants 60-strong chain of shops, but come 2000 Fuller's decided to sell them to the South East-based chain of off-licences, Unwins.

A statement at the time explained the reasons: 'Owing to Unwins' larger scale of operations, Fuller's is confident that this course of action will give its wine shops and staff the best opportunity to flourish in the future. Most of the employees affected will be retained by Unwins and the company has also undertaken to retail Fuller's ale throughout its estate under a five-year agreement. Both boards believe that this transaction will result in a wine shop chain that reflects the best attributes of both companies.'

Michael Turner recalls that, 'in 2000 we sold the wine retailing side to Unwins as we felt that the supermarkets were getting better at wine. We sold it at a time when we had a good price for it and then reinvested the money in hotels. The City thought it was a bad idea but then we are prepared to be different and stand up on our own. When the Beer Orders came along we had a lot of pressure to either become a brewery or retailer and if we became a retailer to pick between tenanted or managed. We said we would

continue being vertically integrated. We are permanently being told off by the City. They think we are eccentric and view me as awkward. We don't do what they expect.'

What beer drinkers perhaps didn't expect in 2000 was the launch of two new beers from Fuller's, both very different from each other though both had been available before in different formats and markets. First of all, there was London Porter, which up until then had been an export-only brand. The launch on the home market came in the wake of the beer's gold medal in the previous year's International Food and Drink competition. The other beer to be launched (or relaunched) was Organic Honey Dew (it had previously been non-organic). By now John Keeling was head brewer, with Reg Drury having retired in 1999. He recalls how the relaunch was tied in with the growing interest in organic beers.

HONEY DEW WAS RELAUNCHED AS AN ORGANIC BEER IN 2000, WHILE THE SAME YEAR SAW LONDON PORTER BECOME AVAILABLE IN THE HOME MARKET

GALES HSB, A CLASSIC ENGLISH ALE AND STILL BEING BREWED

excited lovers of the beer, one of whom had travelled all the way from San Francisco to try it.

In 2000, Anthony Fuller was also chairman of the Independent Family Brewers of Britain, which had been formed in 1993. Fuller's has always been a strong and active member of the organisation, which continues to ensure that the needs and opinions of the smaller independent brewers are fairly heard in government circles at home and in Europe. In an interview, he recalled the tumultuous times that had followed the Beer Orders: 'Some of us thought the Brewers' Society would fall apart because of the effects of the Beer Orders. As a family company we wanted to be part of an organisation that took a different view of the industry than the Brewers' Society could, and also which explained our particular problems as independent family brewers to politicians and officials in Westminster and Brussels.'

There was more change coming for Fuller in 2002 when he stood down as chairman of Fuller, Smith & Turner, having spent 20 years in the position.

'Originally it was Reg's idea to use honey and then under me it became an organic beer. We wanted to explore the organic category, but after a couple of years we realised that the category wasn't going to grow that big so none of our other beers are organic, though Honey Dew still is. However, it did give us an insight into the organic world and it's a good, refreshing beer. A beer is about refreshment, character and satisfaction. For instance, Chiswick is more about refreshment while 1845 about character.'

Despite being retired, Reg Drury had kept busy. In the same year he wrote about his experiences as a judge at the Great American Beer Festival in Denver the previous autumn. Naturally, as someone who had brewed ESB for more years than he could remember, one of the beer styles he was asked to judge was the extra special bitter category. 'To judge some of the 46 ESBs entered was a particular pleasure for me given the heritage of this category,' he wrote. He had also been a special guest at Denver's famous Falling Rock Tap House, where he'd poured pints of cask ESB to

BRANCHING OUT: FOLLOWING THE ACQUISITION OF GALES IN 2005 (BELOW), FULLER'S HAS ALSO PURCHASED CORNISH ORCHARDS, OPENED LONDON'S PRIDE AT HEATHROW TERMINAL 2 AND ACQUIRED A 51 PER CENT SHARE OF CIDER AND PIZZA RESTAURANT BUSINESS, THE STABLE (RIGHT)

# FAMILY VALUES

FULLER, SMITH & TURNER IS A FAMILY BREWERY whose values include a long-term focus; a culture of style over fashion; a passion for quality; premium products (both pubs and beer) and pride in their brands and people. When we think of the people and the pride that the brewery has in them it's no surprise to discover that many – even in these shiftless and rootless times – have spent their working lives with the company. Take Brendan Bray, for instance. He was Fuller's longest-standing member of staff who retired during the summer of 2015 and had been with the company for 49 years since joining as a brewing room boy in 1966. What is remarkable about Bray's retirement is that he was just one of many who have not worked anywhere else – and, given the brewery's location within the community, there are several families who have worked at Fuller's, whether in the brewery or in pubs, down through the generations. According to Chris Hooper, herself described as a long-serving receptionist and post-room manager, 'The Lockie family has spent 250 years in all at Fuller's and have included Old Jim, Kate, Young Jim, Eric, plus an uncle from Wood Street. Young Jim is still alive. There are other families, the Prices, the Powells and the Huxleys and MacNamaras. In fact, we used to be known as the wedding bureau or marriage agency as many people met and married their partners here.' Family values indeed.

Michael Turner, who was then managing director, took on the role of chief executive.

One of Turner's (and the company's) biggest challenges came in 2005 when the respected Hampshire brewery George Gale was acquired and integrated. Based in Horndean and founded in 1847 (making it two years younger than Fuller's), Gales was noted for beers such as HSB, Butser and Prize Old Ale, this last one a classic barley wine packaged in a corked 'nip' bottle. The deal was worth £82.7 million and, according to Michael Turner and the managing director of Gales, Nigel Atkinson, both of whom were interviewed in Fuller's house magazine *The Griffin*, the deal was struck in the Still & West in Old Portsmouth, after the two of them had been out and about looking at pubs in the area.

'I asked him if he was serious,' Atkinson was quoted as saying, 'and it all progressed from there.' He went back to the brewery's shareholders and eventually a price was agreed.

'Gales is the perfect fit for Fuller's,' said Turner, 'it has a great estate of quality pubs and excellent beer brands. Our estate is mainly comprised of freehold properties, as is nearly all the Gales estate. The pubs are well managed, well invested and well looked after, and the cultures and values of Gales are very similar to our own – which should make it much easier to bring the two companies together.

'We have been looking at businesses for the last ten years and had an in-depth look at around 12 in particular. Gales came top of the list of our targets because we liked everything they do, and feel that emotionally they are closer to Fuller's than anyone else. Size is becoming ever more important, and it is the right moment for both Fuller's and Gales to come together. We will be stronger due to the union.'

The purchase brought with it 111 Gales pubs, which lifted Fuller's total estate to 362. As for the beers, Gales Brewery's maximum capacity was 50,000 barrels, which meant that its output could easily be accommodated within Fuller's 260,000-barrel limit. This resulted in the closure of the Horndean brewery, though the beers were saved and, thanks to some very close matching under the keen eye of John Keeling, the name and many of the beers still survive today. Fuller's also bought a new site close to the old brewery and built a brand-new distribution centre.

TEN YEARS AFTER THE EVENT, Michael Turner recalled the acquisition as 'a game-changing moment in our history. It was a good deal for their shareholders, and it was a good deal for Fuller's too. They had reached a stage where the family was no longer actively engaged in the running of the business, and they sold out at the top of the market. It was also good timing for us as they had a quality estate of pubs that were an excellent geographical fit for us, and we were able to invest in all of them, which enhanced our returns. We had made a number of brewery acquisitions but none for the previous 100 years. It was a big challenge to integrate the two companies, and cultures, but the whole team threw themselves into their new challenge, and did an outstanding job very swiftly.'

Another person with proud memories of the work done to integrate the two companies after the purchase is Simon Emeny, currently Fuller's chief executive. The first non-family member in this role when he was appointed in 2013, he has been with the company since 1996 and joined the main board two years later. He recalls the positive aspects of the Gales acquisition. 'Buying Gales gave us more geographical reach,' he says now, 'and it gave us confidence as a business. We had to integrate a business and we had never had to do it before. But we did it and over-delivered. That has given us confidence to successfully expand our estate even further and acquire Cornish Orchards, the Heathrow Terminal 2 pub and a 51 per cent share in the craft cider and pizza restaurant business, The Stable. The Gales deal was really transforming.

'As for the beers, the CAMRA people trusted us to do the right thing, which we did. We spent a lot of time matching the brews and reinvested in the Gales pubs.'

AS WELL AS BEING KEPT BUSY working on the Gales beers, John Keeling was also following a new project, which would eventually become the Brewer's Reserve collection. At the time, breweries in both the USA and the UK were experimenting with ageing beers in various casks, some of which had once held whisky or brandy. The seeds were sown when Keeling visited a friend who worked at Glenmorangie and began to wonder what would happen if he put beer into casks used by the distillery. He was sent some Glenmorangie and Jim Beam casks and decided to experiment with a combination of

## SUPPORT, CHARITIES AND SPONSORSHIP

FULLER, SMITH & TURNER has always prided itself on being part of the local community, which as Richard Fuller says 'means that as a company we support local charities'. Sponsorship is also undertaken for a variety of activities, which unsurprisingly, given the proximity to the river, includes the Fuller's Head of the River Fours, which the company started sponsoring in 1979. Naturally, those who wish to watch the Oxford and Cambridge Boat Race will find the Fuller's-owned Dove and the Fulham Reach-located Blue Boat ideal vantage points with a glass of London Pride to hand.

Golden Pride and Vintage. After leaving them for several months, he tasted and analysed the strength of the beer – because finished whisky casks still have some spirit in them, the so-called Angels' Share, the strength of the beer had increased by 3%.

At the time, he wrote about the experience: 'I thought the beers were superb. I thought it might be a good idea to contact Her Majesty's Revenue & Customs. They advised me that if a beer picks up more than 0.5% ABV it would be classed as a spirit and therefore liable to spirit duty. I countered this by saying that part of the pick-up was secondary fermentation and in any case we could dilute with more beer to avoid spirit payment. This seemed to satisfy them. Marketing targeted me with an ABV of 7%. To achieve that, the base beer had to be weaker than the 8.5% Golden Pride. So I picked ESB export at 5.9% and 1845 at 6.3%. I then thought

that we could blend this down to 7%. Bill Lumsden at Glenmorangie distillery kindly sent us some more casks and we were on our way.

'We again talked to customs. They were beginning to have cold feet. They said that if the beer contained more than 0.5% alcohol originally from the whisky, the beer would be classified as a spirit. We would then have to pay spirit duty. To pay spirit duty we would need a spirit licence. To have a spirit licence we needed to own a still and, wait for it... it was illegal for a brewery to own a still! They then decided to speak to customs HQ.

'We were then informed that if whisky was any part of the beer, then it was a spirit. This meant all the beer had to pay spirit duty. However, we could apply for a licence and pay that duty. This would make the beer very expensive.'

**TIME FOR A REST: BEERS AGEING IN WHISKY CASKS, WHICH WILL EVENTUALLY BECOME ANOTHER BEER IN THE BREWER'S RESERVE SERIES**

**WOOD-AGED WONDER: BREWER'S RESERVE – THIS ONE HAS BEEN AGED IN SINGLE MALT CASKS**

HISTORY ON A PAGE: ONE OF FULLER'S BREWING BOOKS, WHICH CAPTURE THE ESSENCE OF EVERY BEER BREWED SINCE THE 19TH CENTURY

This was part of a talk that Keeling gave to the British Guild of Beer Writers, which had organised a seminar on wood-aged beers in the autumn of 2007. He brought three beers to the event, an ESB whisky beer (8.5%), an 1845 whisky beer (8.75%) and a blended whisky beer (7%), but there still remained the problem with Customs and Excise. Fortunately, the logjam was eventually broken and the first in the series was released in 2008, a 7.7% beer that had spent 500 days in 30-year-old single malt casks. Three others have followed, with the use of Cognac, Auchentoshan and Armagnac casks. These are all superb beers that show off the skill of Keeling's brewing team as well as Fuller's open-minded approach to experimentation.

'Brewer's Reserve was a fantastic thing to do,' says Keeling. 'Here you have far more permission to experiment and make different beers, though I am also very proud of keeping the consistency of London Pride. I came here in 1981 after starting in Wilson's Brewery in Manchester and Fuller's suited my character and individuality. When I joined Fuller's, its management culture philosophy was the opposite of Wilson's. Fuller's was about wanting people to be more individualistic, while

at Wilson's you had to fit into a box. I always thought that if I had stayed at Wilson's I would have become a different brewer.'

This dedication to exploration and innovation bore fruit in another ground-breaking beer series, Past Masters, which began life in 2011 with XX Strong Ale from 1891. According to Keeling, 'I was thinking that there is all this craft beer stuff going on and we can learn from it. There are things we can do better than they do; for instance, if you brew a beer from the past we can do it better, we have the recipe, the methodology and we are brewing in the same place. One of the most satisfying things to do is, say, brew an 1893 Double Stout in the same place it was brewed in the 19th century.'

FULLER'S ZEAL FOR BEEFING UP THE PUB ESTATE continued as well. In 2009, it paid Punch Taverns £21.1 million for six Spirit Group pubs in central London. These included the Red Lion on Parliament Street, which is popular with MPs, and the Grade II-listed Ye Olde Mitre in Hatton Garden. At the time, Michael Turner was quoted as saying, 'These are exceptional quality assets that fit well into our existing portfolio and

A ROYAL VISIT: THE PRINCE OF WALES AND DUCHESS OF CORNWALL AT THE PARCEL YARD IN 2013 WITH MANAGER NICK CAMERON

we will move sympathetically to fold each pub's unique character and heritage into Fuller's. We continue to build our business for the long term and hope existing and new customers will come and enjoy these pubs for many years.'

The same year also saw the acquisition of three Mitchells & Butlers pubs plus the Holly Bush in Hampstead. Now Michael Turner looks back and muses on these acquisitions: 'If we want to make the pubs a success, we have to do them better than other people. The emphasis on quality is essential – 20 years ago we developed the theme of Quality, Service and Pride. That still stands today. Every company says they do quality but you have to get the whole team to believe in it.'

As the new decade sped on, Fuller's wowed drinkers with a series of other pubs. The Union Tavern in Westbourne Grove was formerly a gastro-pub but then had a makeover and relaunch in 2012, with stripped-down oak floorboards, plenty of light and old-school pub tables with clawed feet. What really made it stand out was the excellent food and the choice of beers – as well as Fuller's beers it had offerings from the new

generation of London craft breweries, both cask and keg (by now there was a new wave of keg that was finding favour with beer geeks). This sense of collaboration with other London breweries is a common theme in the way Fuller's conducts its business. 'We have always been open,' says John Keeling, 'we have always encouraged our brewers to be open to other brewers; we show brewers around. If there is a micro-brewer who wants to learn to make beer, we can fit them in. After all, we are founder members of the London Brewers' Alliance. We are gregarious brewers, we are not insular brewers – we like to get out and like to mix.'

The Parcel Yard at King's Cross was another stunning pub success. Formerly, as the name might suggest, a parcel sorting office, it opened in 2012 at the northern end of the King's Cross concourse, close to where tourists queue up to be photographed opposite the entrance to Harry Potter's Platform 9¾. It is spread over two floors and is Fuller's largest pub, with a site measuring 10,000 square feet. A year after its opening, it was voted Fuller's Pub of the Year, and in 2014 it won Best Individual Food and Beverage Concept at a Rail

# THE FUTURE: CHALLENGES AND OPPORTUNITIES

### MICHAEL TURNER – CHAIRMAN

When I became managing director in 1992, my chairman Anthony Fuller and I ran the business together. He was definitely the boss, but over time the responsibility transferred to me, and I was fortunate enough to inherit the trust of the shareholders from Anthony. For several years Simon and I have been working closely as a team. He is now in charge, and represents the future of the business. The aims and ambitions of the business remain the same, but the manner in which the strategy is implemented has been refreshed. If someone is in charge for a long time the company begins to think the way that person has taught them. After 20 years it was time for some fresh thinking and leadership from Simon, and my role now as the chairman of the family business is to keep an eye on things.

### SIMON EMENY – CHIEF EXECUTIVE

Our reputation both as a company and as a brand is critical to us in all communities, whether they be our customers, our colleagues or our investors, and in today's competitive and socially connected world we have to work hard in new ways to build the company we love. In recent years our pub estate has evolved superbly to grow its popularity, especially around food and service. In the past customers saw a pub as a place to drink; today it remains a social hub, but increasingly it is also a place to eat as a family, chat over a coffee, celebrate and stay overnight. Times have changed and I am proud of the way Fuller's has evolved to lead our industry.

### RICHARD FULLER – DIRECTOR

We have a good business model that needs to be flexible, but it is all about quality investments. Because Fuller's is also a broad-based business, it means that if one element doesn't have a good year, you have another part of the company that makes up for it. The challenges we face going forward will be recruiting and retaining top quality people, keeping a long-term focus and keeping our shareholders happy.

As a family business our culture and values are hugely important. Everyone wants to make sure that we retain our independence for many years to come, and our long-term vision and strategy, together with the quality of our people and investments, should ensure this.

Station at the International Food and Beverage Creative Excellence Awards. At the start of 2013 it received a different sort of accolade when the Prince of Wales and Duchess of Cornwall dropped in for a visit.

If you ask Simon Emeny about Fuller's philosophy, the answer suggests he could be talking about the Parcel Yard. 'It is to exploit high quality niches in the marketplace and to do what we do with great style, personality and quality. We are primarily interested in the long term and we see ourselves as custodians of the company; we have to drive the bus on for the long term and take everyone with us. In the future we will continue to go forward in the same vein, continuing our philosophy, remaining independent and investing in our pubs and our brands. My challenge is to retain everything that has made this company so successful, and to reach an even higher level. We have got some very talented people coming through and we are buying some wonderful pubs so we can go forward.'

In 2013, Fuller's took themselves in a different direction when they bought a small Cornish cider company for £3.8 million. It was the brewery's first foray into the cider market and at the time Simon Emeny said: 'We are delighted to have purchased Cornish Orchards, a company we admire. We have been brewing beer for over 160 years and, like Cornish Orchards, understand the importance of quality. Our commitment to Cornwall, Cornish products and Cornish jobs is paramount. We will help the passionate team at Westnorth Manor Farm, Duloe, grow production and sales of their wonderful Cornish products, helping to take them to new markets.'

The world of beer and hospitality has changed immensely in the past ten years. Who would have thought that people could tweet John Keeling about a Fuller's beer that they were drinking on the other side of the world? Social media has opened up the sector, with the aid of blogs and reviewing websites (not always advantageous, it has to be said). The strength of Fuller, Smith & Turner is its survival as a family brewery (though sadly there are no more Smiths involved), and Michael Turner explains: 'When you join somewhere like this you think you are going to be here for such a short

THE ROMANCE OF THE PUB: A PERFORMANCE OF *ROMEO AND JULIET* IN ONE OF FULLER'S PUBS

period in the life of the company and you think you won't make a difference to its history. I had no concept that the company would remain independent through half my working life, let alone through all of it. Starting with my uncle and then Anthony Fuller, they changed the business and started growing it, and now everyone expects us to remain independent. For the future you need some members of the family to be involved, but they have to be really talented, very able, and they have to be leaders.'

For Richard Fuller, the heritage is very important, 'but you need to be looking forward all the time. Enzo Ferrari said you should always look back so you don't make the same mistakes going forward. It's getting the balance between the roots and foundation and a forward-looking culture. I remember some years ago listening to someone who was talking about Japanese companies and their strategies – this person had done a lot of work out in Japan, and told a story about how at a famous company the hosts had pulled out a document that was 150 years old, which still guided them.'

As for the future, Simon Emeny is positive and brimming with confidence. 'We recruit people who enjoy working as part of a team, have a positive outlook on life, a rounded personality. People chat to each other and support colleagues here. While I want to maintain the things that have made it so successful, I also want to make my own mark. Using football as an analogy, I would say that there are many ways of winning the Premier League but we are only interested in winning with great style. I don't want record profits by taking short cuts. I want to win the Premier League with stylish football.

'During 2015 some of our pubs have welcomed a touring production of *Romeo and Juliet*. I suspect if you took a hard-nosed view it doesn't make any money but our customers love it; it means we connect with them. I see non-stop challenges, which is why businesses like ours have to keep pushing themselves. For instance, people's drinking habits have changed, and there is a need to manage diets and drinking differently. Then there is the role of technology and social media for today's generation and its role in how they live their lives and our business is adapting well to this. Society is changing far faster than it has ever done in the past and we have to move

with the times. Take the new wave of keg beers. They are fantastic and are able to combine flavour with the right temperature.

'We have to keep innovating, but that can be fun. Business has to be fun here. I have been here 19 years and I am still excited every day.'

HISTORY AND HERITAGE can sometimes be a millstone, keeping companies and individuals static and stifling forward progress. In the 170 years that beer has been brewed under the name of Fuller, Smith & Turner, the people who have come and gone have not allowed the past to stop them from taking the business forward. Whether it was the guiding hand of GP Fuller, the forceful advice of Dr Moritz, the astuteness of Anthony Fuller and then Michael Turner, or the brewing prowess of Reg Drury and then John Keeling, the history of Fuller, Smith & Turner is one of remarkable people taking the right decisions at the right time.

Fuller, Smith & Turner will be around and making great beer and running marvellous pubs, hotels and bars for a long time to come yet. The founding fathers can rest easy.

# FULLER'S PUB PROFILE
## The Blue Boat

THIS IS ONE OF FULLER'S NEWEST PUBS and was opened in March 2015 by twice world champion and Olympic bronze medal-winning rower, Sarah Winckless. Sitting on the Thames, the Blue Boat is part of the riverside development Fulham Reach, and it's a modern and comfortable place where drinkers and diners can watch time and the river pass on by, idle and idyllic, with a gleaming pint of London Pride or Oliver's Island to hand. Those wanting to ramp up the action a bit will also find it the perfect place to cheer on the hardy rowers of the Boat Race as they pass by in the spring sunshine. Inside, the interior is a mixture of recycled wood, chrome, nautical styling, bookshelves and a sprinkling of booths that wouldn't go amiss in an American diner. However, the most striking effect is of lightness and airiness, a sprightly, brightly lit place that along with the great drink and food makes up a trinity of joy. Meanwhile, great beers (cask and modern keg) and wine share equal billing, while the kitchen produces a changing menu of seasonal and judiciously sourced produce – how about some sea trout or a 32-day aged bone-in Hampshire sirloin steak followed by a Vintage Ale sticky toffee pudding? Thought so.

THE BLUE BOAT, DISTILLERY WHARF, PARR'S WAY, LONDON W6 9GD

# TASTING NOTE

## FRONTIER, 4.5%

FRONTIER WAS LAUNCHED IN 2013 as a 'new wave craft lager'. In the words of John Keeling: 'With Frontier we are producing a new style of lager, which is actually brewed like a Kölsch. My reasoning behind it: I was so tired of standard lager being one dimensional in flavour so I thought, let's make it more flavoursome – Frontier is one beer I want to succeed more than any of the others. We have done things our way. It is not a traditional lager; it is our own interpretation of a lager, using US hops and ale yeast and being lagered for a decent time. We did all this for flavour rather than any other reason. We also wanted to add a modern tweak to it as well and therefore used US hops, and because we wanted to really mature (or lager) it, we lagered for six weeks. With Frontier I want to make a beer that everyone can drink. It's not a beer that is made for any one fragment of the market. I want people to walk into a wedding reception and see three commonplace beer brands and there's Frontier and they will make for that. It's not meant to be anything other than a beer to enjoy.'

Gleams golden in the glass with effusive fruity notes leaping out, suggestive of citrus, passion fruit and melon; it is clean and refreshing on the palate with a sweep of tropical fruit before finishing dry and crisp.

# Whole Grilled Lemon Sole with Tartare Sauce, Chips and Watercress

Serves 4

## INGREDIENTS

| | |
|---|---|
| 4 | 280–340g lemon sole (ask your fishmonger to leave the head on and remove the dark top skin) |
| 1 tsp | butter, softened, plus extra for greasing |

For the tartare sauce:

| | |
|---|---|
| 40g | baby capers, finely chopped |
| 40g | gherkins, finely chopped |
| 1 | red onion, finely diced |
| 20g | finely chopped fresh dill |
| 280g | mayonnaise |
| juice and zest of 1 lemon |
| salt and ground white pepper |

For the crispy chips:

| | |
|---|---|
| 1.5kg | potatoes (we use Potato Lovers), peeled and cut into chips |
| vegetable oil, for frying, plus extra for greasing |

To garnish:

| | |
|---|---|
| 2 | lemons, halved |
| fresh watercress |

## METHOD

To prepare the tartare sauce, put the capers and gherkins in a bowl and add the dill and red onion. Add the lemon juice and zest, and the mayonnaise. Combine until well mixed, season to taste and set aside in the fridge until ready to use.

Blanch the chipped potatoes in a fryer set at 150°C for 5 minutes, then allow to cool.

Preheat the grill on high. Place the lemon sole whole on a buttered and oiled tray, season with a little salt and a teaspoon of soft butter, and place under the grill for 10–15 minutes, until the skin is a nice light golden colour and the flesh cooked through.

While the fish is cooking, cook the chips again in the fryer set at 180°C, then drain and season.

Gently remove the cooked sole from the tray using a fish slice and serve with a spoonful of tartare sauce and a portion of crispy chips. Garnish with half a lemon and some fresh watercress.

# TASTING NOTES

BEER NAME

ABV

COLOUR

AROMA

TASTE

FINISH


BEER NAME

ABV

COLOUR

AROMA

TASTE

FINISH


BEER NAME

ABV

COLOUR

AROMA

TASTE

FINISH


BEER NAME

ABV

COLOUR

AROMA

TASTE

FINISH

# WRITE YOUR OWN TASTING NOTES FOR YOUR FAVOURITE FULLER'S BEERS

BEER NAME _____

ABV _____

COLOUR _____

AROMA _____

TASTE _____

FINISH _____


BEER NAME _____

ABV _____

COLOUR _____

AROMA _____

TASTE _____

FINISH _____


BEER NAME _____

ABV _____

COLOUR _____

AROMA _____

TASTE _____

FINISH _____


BEER NAME _____

ABV _____

COLOUR _____

AROMA _____

TASTE _____

FINISH _____

# ACKNOWLEDGEMENTS

A CIP catalogue record for the book is available from the British Library
ISBN  978-0-9934615-0-7

Cover and book design and art direction by Lisa David          www.lisadaviddesign.com
Cover and main book photography by Thomas Skovsende          www.thomasskovsende.com
Printed and bound by DZS Grafik in Ljubljana, Slovenia          www.dzs-grafik.si

Written by Adrian Tierney-Jones
Adapted from the original publication 'London Pride: 150 Years of Fuller Smith and Turner 1845 – 1995',
by Andrew Langley

Recipes by Paul Dickinson, Head of Food, and Gavin Sinden, Fuller, Smith & Turner PLC

Thanks to Lisa Gaywood for her dedication in searching through the Fuller's archives
Thanks to Ian Strang and Little Scotney Farm in Tunbridge Wells for access to their wonderful hop farm, and for
supplying Fuller, Smith & Turner with quality hops for many years

Acknowledgments:

*page 10*      Matthias Mawson portrait appears with the kind permission of the Master and Fellows of Corpus Christi
               College, Cambridge
*page 28*      Jacob Knyff's painting 'Chiswick from the river' is reproduced by courtesy of the Museum of London
*page 40*      Turnham Green Station photograph © TfL from the London Transport Museum collection
*page 59*      Dr Moritz photograph, courtesy of the Institute of Brewing and Distilling
*page 67*      Isleworth brewery door photograph © Leslie Bailey, courtesy of the Brewery History Society
*page 96*      CAMRA logo courtesy of the Campaign For Real Ale
*page 101*     Image of Marmite © Thomas Skovsende, permission to use product courtesy of Unilever

Published by Fuller, Smith and Turner P.L.C